Amusing Artistry in Polymer Clay:

Blue Seabird Clay Designs

Helen Cruickshank

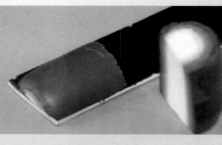

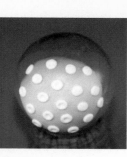

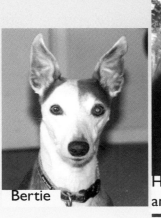

Bertie

Helen with Blue and Persie

Millie

Amusing Artistry in Polymer Clay:

Blue Seabird Clay Designs

- 9 Projects •
- Step-by-step instructions • 14 Cane designs •
- Techniques Scope for own designs •

Helen Cruickshank.

First published 2018   Blue Seabird Clay Designs
helen.cruickshank@blueseabirdclaydesigns.co.uk   Blue Seabird Clay Designs on Facebook

Every effort has been made to ensure that all information in this book is accurate. However, due to differing conditions, tools, and individual skills, the publisher cannot be responsible for any injuries, losses, or other damages that may result from the use of the information in this book.

While polymer clay is branded as non-toxic and safe when used correctly, it is advisable to follow certain guidelines: do not eat it, do not let baked or unbaked polymer clay come in contact with food, wash your hands after using polymer clay, use clay-dedicated tools, avoid burning polymer clay by following the clay manufacturers' recommended baking temperatures and times, and supervise children who are using polymer clay. Use extreme caution when working with any tools with sharp edges or points, such as the tissue blades or needle tools, to avoid injury. Always supervise children who used sharp tools.

ISBN : 978-1-5272-2027-0

This book is dedicated to
my husband, Iain.

For putting up with my clay taking over the house.

For pretending to look at every single thing I make,

and oohing in the right places.

And pouring the wine!

Acknowledgements:

There are so many people who have inspired and/or helped me to write this book. Tracy Marriott, my clay buddy and great friend, I've had so many wonderful evenings with you experimenting with clay; I love your enthusiasm and encouragement, and talent. My sister Ruth, who imitates the seagulls in Finding Nemo with her cries of 'mine, mine, mine' whenever I post pictures of my creations on facebook - you really are a huge support and boost to my confidence, and who always has my back. My daughter Emma, who has followed in my footsteps and become an Occupational Therapist, who understands the complicated working of my obsessive brain and un-muddles it, who proof read many of the tutorials, and of whom I'm inordinately proud.

To my mother who always shows interest and enthusiasm in anything I do, and makes everyone who knows her feel special; and my father who gave me the belief that anything is possible, and has just learnt to fly a plane at the age of 82. Also to my nephew Jack who is always so complimentary about my clay, even the dubious looking attempts at dragons!

To Frank Fisher and Angie Scarr for encouraging me to write the book in the first place, and a huge thank you in particular to Frank who has been my go-to advisor and support over navigating the bewildering and baffling world of self-publishing and Scribus - your unstinting, knowledgeable and generous support has made this book possible.

To my clay group: Linda Hyam, Ruth Peck, Tracy Marriot, and Belinda Elliott for their enthusiasm of my designs, willingness to be my guinea pigs for all new tutorials, and their love of clay, which makes Tuesday nights my favourite night of the week. To Birdy Heywood who started me on using a pasta machine and initiated my love of caning, to all the wonderful tutors and artists I've had the good fortune to attend workshops with and who are so generous in sharing their knowledge: Marie Segal, Carol Simmons, Nikolina Orson, Melanie Muir, Doreen Gay Kassell, Jana Roberts Benzon, Angie Scarr, Karen Walker and Cara Jane Hayman.

A special thank you to Penny Vingoe of ClayAround, who encourages me, nags me, challenges me, and who is one of those people that I wish I'd met years ago. Not only is she a friend, but she is the best supplier of polymer clay and a huge variety of clay accessories and tools I know. To Donna Barratta, another one of those wonderful people who I met through claying, and has become a firm friend, and who proof read my tuturials for me at the point I was sick of them!

To my college friends Judith, Sadie, Erika and Angela who taught me about things like domains, and offered to trial the tutorials, (and even more of a thank you for not going ahead with it!). And last but by no means least, to all my friends, both clayers and non-clayers who have been so enthusiastic about my book, and had faith in my ability to write it even when I didn't.

I am an Occupational Therapist working in Mental Health. As Occupational Therapy uses meaningful activities to motivate and help people overcome barriers to everyday life, my discovery of polymer clay was almost inevitable. I found a half price pack of small blocks of Fimo clay and took it to work for one of my anxiety groups to make beads with; they loved it, but I found an obsession!

I made some liquorice-style beads and made them into a necklace, then spent the next year modelling fruit, vegetables, leaves, in fact anything I could think of, into beads. My friend Linda showed me a pendant she'd bought from Birdy Heywood; I was blown away by what could be achieved in polymer clay, so looked her up, went for a lesson, and knew that I'd found something special that I wanted to explore fully.

Over the past 4-5 years I've soaked up as much information and advice as work and family commitments allow. During this time I have brought reindeers, chickens, ponies, turtles, robins, parrots and dogs into creatiion, alongside my beads in all shapes, sizes and designs. I have practiced every technique I can get my hands on in a bid to constantly be looking for new and exciting ways of using this wonderful product, although my main love remains making canes, which has fascinated me from the beginning.

Over time my style has evolved into using canes to create more depth and originality in my designs, and it is this style that I hope to share with you in this book, which even complete beginners can achieve. Not only does every design have an easy to follow, step-by-step process, but each one allows the artist to put their own stamp on their creation with endless possibilities.

I hope you enjoy exploring this book as much as I have enjoyed writing it.

> "Imagination is the soul's happiest retreat"
>
> James Lendall Basford (1845-1915)

Contents:

PM7 ??????

Pasta Machine settings:

????? PM5

There are many different pasta machine used for polymer clay, and all have different thicknesses. Not only that, but some machines have the lowest numbers as the thickest settings, and the higher numbers the thinnest, and others have completely the opposite, some have 9 settings, some 7, and so on.

PM3

Therefore, instead of giving instructions such as 'the thickest setting on your pasta machine', I've measured the thickness of each of my Atlas Pasta Machine settings using standard playing cards in order for you to know what thickness I'm using throughout the tutorials.

I've abrieviated each setting to PM0 - 9. PM standing for Pasta Machine, and the number is the setting number. So, PM3 is pasta machine setting 3.

PM0

My pasta machine thicknesses for each setting:
PM0 = 8 standard playing cards
PM1 = 7 standard playing cards
PM2 = 6 standard playing cards
PM3 = 4 standard playing cards
PM4 = 3 standard playing cards
PM5 = 2.5 standard playing cards
PM6 = 2 standard playing cards
PM7 = 1 standard playing card
PM8 & 9 = less than 1 standard playing card

PM6

To find out the thicknesses of the settings on the pasta machine you're using:

• First put your pasta machine on the thickest setting
• Put a few standard playing cards together and put them through the machine.
• Keep adding cards until you have reached the maximum number that can go through in one pass
• Write this down, then continue for all the settings on your machine
• Then compare your machine thicknesses with mine
• For example: If my PM6 is 2 cards thick, but your PM5 is 2 cards thick, every time you see PM6, you will use

Health and Safety - boring but important information!

CAUTION - SHARP TOOLS:
The instructions in this book include the use of knives, tissue blades, cocktail sticks, needle tools and other sharp instruments. Using sharp tools may result in injury; use with extreme care, keep out of reach of children, and supervise young people.

IS CLAY TOXIC?
Many people are concerned about the toxicity of polymer clay. Ginger Davis Allman of The Blue Bottle Tree wrote an excellent article on the safety of polymer clay, it can be found at https://thebluebottletree.com/polymer-clay-safe/. Safety information by Polyform, who make Sculpey and Premo clay, can also be found at www.sculpey.com.

GETTING STARTED WITH POLYMER CLAY:

Polymer Clay is a synthetic modelling material that remains flexible until it is cured by baking at a low temperature in a normal oven. It doesn't dry out at room temperature, is made from a basis of PVC resin and a liquid plasticizer, and can be shaped and re-shaped without deterioration. It is perfect for everyone, from beginners to professional artists, and there really is no limit to the designs and projects you can make with it.   The only limit is your imagination!

The clay used in this book:

There are several types of polymer clay, but the ones I use most, and throughout this book, are Fimo Professional and Premo Sculpey. In a nutshell, this is a synopsis of, in my opinion, some of the most easily available clays:

- **Fimo Professional** (85g/3oz & 350g/12.34oz blocks)
  exceptionally versatile clay, strong when cured, suitable for all projects especially cane work. The only drawback is that it takes longer to condition. One of my favourite clays for canes.

- **Fimo Soft** - (57g/2oz blocks) soft and easy to condition and use, ideal for children and modelling but far too soft for cane making. This is the clay that's the most easy to buy in craft shops.

- **Fimo Effects** (57g/2oz blocks) - comes in 8 different effects: pearl, nightglow (florescent), glitter, translucent, stone, metallic, pastel & gemstone. Great to use on their own or mixed with other clay.

- **Premo Sculpey** (57g/2oz, 227g/8oz & 454g/1lb blocks) - fantastic range of colours, the larger size blocks are in selected colours only. This is my other favourite clay, it's easy to condition but can be too soft for caning if fresh, however, if you leach it (put sheets of clay between paper to 'leech' some of the oil out of the clay) there are no problems. Good for all projects.

- **Premo Sculpey Accents** (57g/2oz & 454g/1lb blocks) - similar to Premo Sculpey and used the same way. Many colours with pearlised, metallic, translucent, granite and glitter effects. Great to use alone or mixed with other clay. I use them extensively throughout this book.

- **Kato Polyclay** (57g/2oz, 354g/12.5oz, and 4 x 1oz blocks in a pack) - this is a wonderful clay for canes, the best I've found. The drawbacks are that it's slightly more expensive, takes longer to condition and has a strong plastic smell which people either seem to love or hate - I love it! It is cured at a slightly higher temperature to Fimo and Premo.

- **Cernit** (56g and 500g blocks) - 34 colours in wonderful categories eg Glamour, Nature, Neon and Doll. I love the colours of Cernit but find it too soft for canes. Wonderful for modelling, look up Karen Walker and see what she creates with Cernit.

Conditioning Polymer Clay:

Polymer clay has to be conditioned (thoroughly mixed) prior to use. Unconditioned clay, even if it appears soft, does not have properly aligned particles and it is important to have the same amount of plasticizers spread evenly throughout your clay. Unconditioned clay that has been cured is more likely to be brittle and break easily. It is very important that before you begin any project that you condition your clay thoroughly. There are two ways to do this, either with your hands or a pasta machine.

1. To use your hands, cut off some clay from the block and roll it between your hands into a ball shape. Next roll it into a long snake or log shape, then back into a ball. Repeat this until the clay doesn't crack or split when you fold it in half.

2. To condition using a pasta machine, cut your block of clay into slices, roll the slices with your clay roller, then put through the pasta machine on the thickest setting. Put two of the slices together and put through the pasta machine again. Fold the clay sheet in half and put through the pasta machine again, with the folded side going through the machine first. Repeat until the clay is pliable and does not crack or split when folded.

Curing your clay pieces:

You will need either your normal oven to cure the clay in, or a separate one if you prefer to keep clay and food separate. I bought a small one for £25 and it works well, although I use my normal oven for larger items such as the pony, reindeer and chicken.

It is really important that you buy an oven and use it all the time. Small ovens in particular tend to 'spike', ie the temperature goes high very quickly, so always pre-heat your oven for around 20 minutes, and wait until the temperature levels out before putting your clay items in.

How I cure Fimo and Premo Sculpey clay.

- Pre-heat the oven on 130°C until the temperature is stable - around 20 minutes
- Place your clay item on a tile and put the tile in an aluminium foil tray. To avoid your clay becoming shiny where it touches the tile, cover the tile with paper.

- Use another foil tray, or a sheet of foil, to cover the clay - this stops the oven's heating element from burning the clay. Alternatively you can put the clay in the oven and cover loosely with foil. It's not essential to cover your clay, I often don't bother, but for important pieces I don't take chances and cover them.
- Instead of the tile, I often cure many of my pieces by filling the tray with cornflower and putting my pieces in it - this stops things rolling away or getting flat and shiny from the tile.

Cure according to clay manufacturer's recommendations.

The basic clay kit:

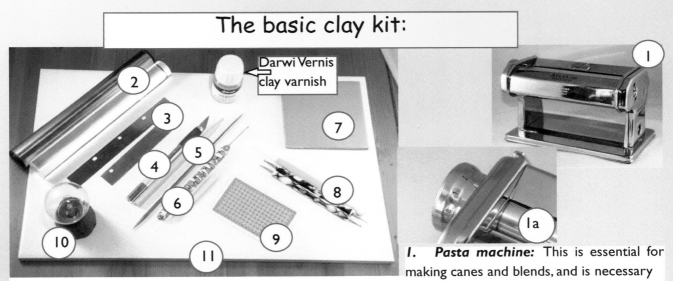

Darwi Vernis clay varnish

1. **Pasta machine:** This is essential for making canes and blends, and is necessary for every project in the book. I have an Atlas Wellbeing 180 which I love, but you don't need an expensive one. Two rollers in the pasta machine squeeze the clay to a sheet of a determined width; the width is adjusted by turning a round gauge on the side (1a).

2. **Acrylic or metal roller:** For flattening and smoothing the clay, especially before putting through the pasta machine, when lengthening square canes, and smoothing surfaces.

3. **Clay blades - flexible and rigid:** The flexible blades (often called tissue blades) tend to be sharper than the rigid ones and are used mostly to cut thin slices from canes. The rigid blades are useful when you need to make a straight cut in a cane, without distorting.

4. **Craft knife:** This little knife has lots of uses; cutting round templates and trimming edges etc

5. **Pointed tools:** I use various sized knitting needles and cable needles, the larger needles are useful to smooth uneven clay, and the smaller ones have numerous uses.

6. **Needle tool:** When you buy this it has a wood or metal handle, I just covered mine with clay. This has many uses, including making holes and texturing.

7. **Small tile:** I buy these from a large DIY shop and they cost around 20p each. Useful for putting individual projects on to work on, then later cure on.

8. **Ball tools of various sizes:** Used to put round indentations in clay. I find many uses for these.

9. **A standard playing card, or a piece of card 9cm x 6cm:** This is my go-to template for making Skinner blends. As I enjoy making canes so much, I don't like making huge ones, and the playing card is just the right size to make a blend that makes a cane large enough for most of my projects.

10. **A light bulb:** This is not actually essential, but so useful for making curved rounded pieces. Cover the bottom of the bulb with clay to make it stand up, or use a cut off cardboard roll (eg toilet roll) which also works well.

11. **A ceramic tile to work on:** You don't need one as large as the one in the picture.

Other tools and materials :

I use many different shapes and sizes of cutters, but the most useful ones are the circles. Kemper Kutters are my favourite as they have a little plunger to push the clay out if it gets stuck. Other useful shapes are ovals, hearts, stars, squares, flowers and leaves. The three size set of circles, 2cm, 3cm & 4cm are essential in the tool kit, and reasonably inexpensive to buy.

I use a clear glass cutting board with a plastic sheet of quilters grid taped underneath. I've photographed the board with a large white tile underneath so you can see it more clearly. The quilter grid is in square inches but you'll see that on the bottom I've put a line of centimetres so I have both metric and imperial. The pink pattern on the top left is my guide to making a step cane, and the blue straight line is the width of my pasta machine so when I make larger Skinner blends I cut the clay sheet to the right size.

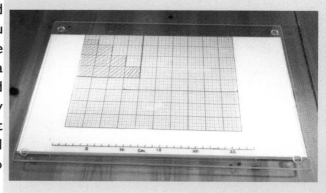

A clay extruder makes long lengths of clay in various shapes. Load clay into the barrel, fix the disc with the hole in the shape of clay you want, turn the handle and voila, lengths of perfectly formed clay! I use it to make clay knitting, canes, edges of pendants, coils, and many other things. Make sure you buy one with a handle, not the very cheap ones that you have to push the clay out manually.

Throughout this book I use Sculpey Bake & Bond clay adhesive, it glues cured clay to non-cured clay. The reason I use the Bake & Bond so often is because many of my projects involve sticking things like cured ears into holes, and the Bake & Bond is liquid, so goes into the holes well. However, my friend Penny Vingoe introduced me to Genesis thick medium extender which is the texture of petrolium jelly (Vaseline) and because it's not a liquid, is very easy to use on flatter pieces. Poly paste, a polymer clay adhesive by Kato is equally as good, so don't feel you have to buy Bake & Bond if you have another clay adhesive.

Often you need to smooth out the surface of your clay, this is called 'burnishing'. To do this lay a piece of thin paper (layout or parchment for example) over your piece and rub something smooth over it. This can be many things, smooth pebble, bone folder, finger etc, but a soapstone (shown left) is inexpensive and perfect for the job.

14

Round-nosed pliers (left): long conical jaws that make rounded bends and loops in wire.

Flat-nosed pliers (middle): flat broad jaws used to grip wire and make sharper bends. I use two pairs in my work as I often grip both ends of a piece of wire and pull to straighten.

Wire cutters (right): as I'm not making jewellery in this book I don't buy expensive wire cutters, anything that will cut 1mm wire.

The Marxit tool is very useful for making evenly spaced marks in clay before cutting slices of equal widths. It has six sides and the marks range from 3mm increments to 20mm. This photo shows my rather grubby but well used Marxit.

Silicone rubber clay shaper tools are useful for making texture in polymer clay and making softer indentations such as in the turtle flippers. They can also be used to smooth over marks in your clay.

A ruler is essential to your polymer clay kit and should have been in the basic clay kit! Make sure you buy a metal one rather than a plastic one as polymer clay can 'melt' certain plastics.

Ultra fine glitter. I use this on canes when I want to highlight the slices such as with the feathers on the owl and chicken. It can also be used to make sheets of shiny clay which can be used in many projects. Make sure you only buy ultra fine glitter as anything larger will result in a grainy surface on your clay.

Gilder's paste can be used to add metallic colour to cured polymer clay. I use various ones, Inca Gold, Pebeo Gilding wax and Creative Expressions Metallic gilding wax. They work particularly well on Steampunk.

Darwi Vernis - Polymer clay varnish and my varnish of choice as it covers evenly and dries in around 15 minutes. There are other polymer clay varnishes available and it is personal choice.

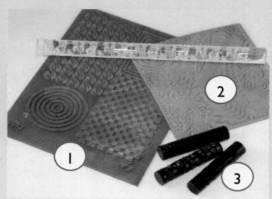

Texture makers. These can be commercial ones such as Helen Breil's (1) and Cernit's (2) texture plates, and the Kor tools (3) and MKM rollers, or you can use items that you probably have round the house such as a toothbrush, pan scrubber, threaded bar, buttons, lace and plastic packing material, or organic materials such as tree bark.

Silicone moulds can be useful. I use them alot in Steampunk, and they are great at decorating items such as tea-lights and spoons, or to enhance a model, for example I made a sea bird and used a fish mould to scatter little silver fish around it. There are absolutely loads of silicone moulds available, sometimes sold for cake decorating, which are also perfect for polymer clay.

Everyone starts somewhere :

This was the first necklace I made; I didn't have a pasta machine, had never even heard of using a pasta machine! and rolled the clay with a pastry roller. This was the start of my clay journey, and I still have this necklace and wear it often. Even though I've made loads more liquorice allsorts necklaces, all with a pasta machine and much better, I kind of like this one best!

After spending a year making all sorts of things into necklaces, I bought a pasta machine. I knew I wanted to make 'different' beads, and these were my first attempts. I keep these and look at them at times when I start to think I should be better, and I they help me realise how far I've come since making them.

Left: This was my first attempt at a chicken, I called it a 'Pidgkin' as it resembled a pigeon more than a chicken!
Right: My first pony, I actually thought that this had a lot of promise, but it still looks like something from the ice age!

TECHNIQUES USED IN THIS BOOK:

SKINNER BLEND

The Skinner Blend was developed by Judith Skinner and is a method of creating a sheet of clay with a graduated blend between two or more colours. It is used extensively throughout this book and gives depth and interest to canes.

Start by rolling out two colours on PM0 and cut to the size of a playing card (9cm x 6cm). For larger Skinner blends make larger rectangles, but this is the size I use for most of my canes.

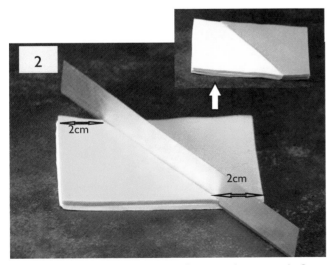

Place one colour on top of the other, mark 2cm from the top left corner and 2cm from the bottom right corner, and cut between the marks. Peel apart the clay and place two of the same colour one side and two of the other colour the other side.

Gently roll the clay with your roller then put it through the pasta machine on PM0, making sure that one colour is to the left, one to the right. Push the clay up to the right hand edge of the pasta machine and keep your left hand on the clay (in this example on the yellow clay) to keep it pressed up against the right hand edge. This will keep the clay from widening too much.

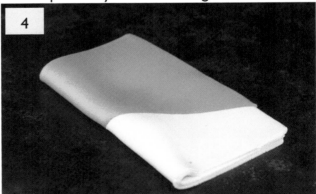

Fold the clay in half, again keeping one colour on the left and one on the right. Put it again through the pasta machine, still on PM0, with the folded side downwards. This prevents air bubbles getting into your clay.

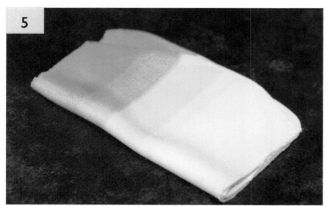

Keep putting your clay through the pasta machine, folding, and repeating. The colours will start blending, don't worry if it looks odd, as long as you keep folding it the right way and putting it through the pasta machine fold down, it will eventually become a lovely smooth blend.

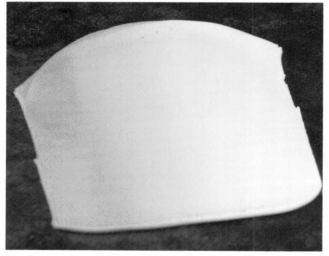

Your finished Skinner blend.

SKINNER BLEND WITH INCREASED DARK BLEND:

I adapted this technique from a tutorial by Ivy Niles, the incredibly talented artist behind iKandiclay. She makes enourmous canes and then reduces them to sizes to sell. Her designs are colourful, intricate and beautiful and I use the cane from her tutorial again and again. One of the reasons her canes are so lovely is because of the depth of her blends, so, I shall stop waffling and show you how I get a similar effect.

Start off following steps 1 and 2 for the Skinner blend then take some black clay and roll it through the pasta machine on a very thin setting, I use PM7.

Cut a piece of black clay the height of the rectangle and 3cm along the bottom edge. Make a curve in the clay from point to point as shown.

Put through the pasta machine following steps 3 to 5 of the Skinner blend and you will end up with a beautiful blend as shown below.

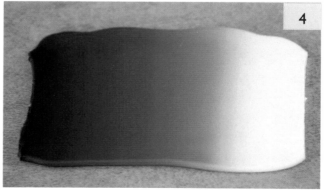

SKINNER BLEND WITH TWO COLOURS THAT DON'T MIX:

Sometimes you want to put two colours together that if mixed, would produce mud. If for example you make red and green into a Skinner blend, the middle part would be a muddy colour - as shown above.

To get round this put a band of white between the two colours.

Top blend is the one without white, the bottom one includes white in the middle.

This is what the two blends look like rolled into a bulls eye cane.

TROUBLESHOOTING UNEVEN OR DISTORTED CLAY:

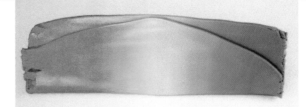

Sometimes you'll find that your clay become shorter one side than the other. I use two different techniques to even it up.

The first way is to fold the clay, and put the side with the shorter clay next to the edge of the pasta machine. With your left hand, push the clay firmly towards the pasta machine edge as it goes through. I tend to swap the clay round regularly as I make a blend.

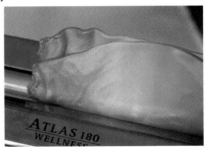

The second way I learnt from Marie Segal. Fold the clay in half as before, then scrunch up the clay where is is shorter. It will come out a very odd shape, but keep putting it through and it will come right.

19

THE MO CLAY METHOD OF MAKING A BLEND:

Monica Resta (Mo Clay) makes wonderful videos of her projects and shares them generously. She has a way of making a blend with only a small amount of clay which only takes a short time, so very useful when making smaller canes.

Start by rolling logs of the clay you want to blend, you can use two or more colours. Roll them to around 6cm each and place next to each other.

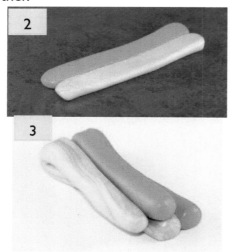

Flatten them a little with your clay roller, then fold the logs in half, off-setting them as shown.

Next push down a little on the clay along the top, then squeeze the long edges, so that you end up with a uniform log, the same width all the way along.

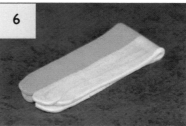

Once you've done this, flatten it with your clay roller and put it through the pasta machine at PM0.

Fold it over, and put it back through the pasta machine again, folded side down. If you want to get a blend even faster you can now put the pasta machine two settings thinner and fold the clay into three as shown to the right. Repeat until you have an even blend. This is different to the Skinner blend as you are left with a long narrower blend.

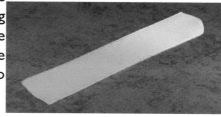

If you want the colours broader, for example if you want to make a bulls eye cane, fold the strip into the width you want, roll gently with your roller, and put through the pasta machine on PM0, one of the colours first (in this example, either orange or cream). This will give you a long strip of the width of cane you want to make.

20

COVERING A CANE WITH ULTRA FINE GLITTER:

Choose your glitter, and put it in a bag. I buy my glitter from Glitter Magic and it comes in handy size bags like the one above. Cut your cane so it will fit into the bag. The glitter has to be ultra fine, anything larger will be gritty.

Close the bag and massage the glitter into the clay. Remove the cane and blow on it to remove the glitter. I like to brush it on my jeans. You want to do all this away from the clay table and only take the cane back when there is no loose glitter.

Now your cane is covered, cut a thin slice off each end, and you will be able to see the cane. This is necessary if you're going to mould the cane into a shape, such as a leaf.

HOW TO ROUND THE END OF A LOG OR CANE:

Many times throughout the book you will see that I've rounded the end of either a cane or a log of clay. Sometimes it's to hide the scrap clay underneath, other times to make a nicer looking end. The example below shows the outside in a different colour to the centre clay which will hopefully make it easier to understand.

To start, using your thumb and first finger gently pinch the edges of the cane inwards. Then repeat on the other two edges, drawing the edges in to cover the scrap clay. Keep moving round the end, pinching gently all the way round until the outside clay meets in the middle. Finally smooth the end to get rid of any uneven parts and your rounded edge is done.

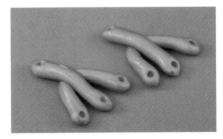

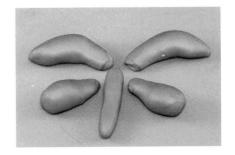

I learnt this very handy technique at a Carol Simmons Master Cane workshop; it minimises the likelihood of an air hole being in the middle of the clay.

Before rolling up the clay, first cut 1cm off the end of your long strip, from the end you want to be in the middle of the cane.

Roll the cut off piece of clay to the width of the strip of clay. Place this on the end of the clay and roll up.

As you can see, no air hole!

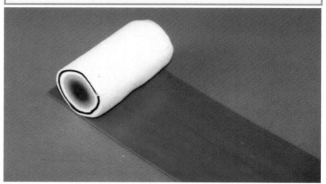

Roll out the clay you want to cover your cane with on PM5, and lay your cane on it. Cut a straight line behind the cane, and two straight lines the width of the cane.

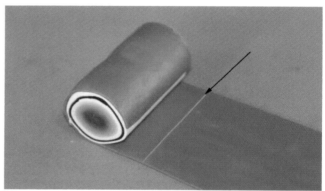

Use your tissue blade to lift the clay behind the cane to start the rolling. Roll completely round, then a little further, before rolling back a little. This will produce a faint line in the clay - I've highlighted it to make it seen more easily - which you then cut along, and roll the cane up again. The two edges will butt together. Finish by rolling the cane gently to smooth out the join and your cane is covered.

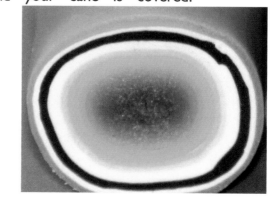

Lavender Bluebell Chicken:

I have had chickens for years. I told my husband around 20 years ago that I'd like some chickens, and he muttered something about the house deeds saying no livestock, and he didn't want any. Needless to say, a few years later I put them on my Christmas wish list, and my sister Ruth bought me three bantams. We've never looked back, and have had chickens ever since. They now have the run of the whole garden! Lavendar Bluebell was one of my favourites; she used to love coming into the house, and even learnt how to get through the fly screen into the kitchen.

The original 3 bantams

TOOLS & MATERIALS:

- Pasta machine
- Acrylic or metal clay roller
- Needle tool / cocktail stick
- Good quality tin foil
- 115cm of 1mm wire – I get it from the garden centre or DIY store
- Circle cutters 3cm diameter (and 1.5mm & approx 7mm for the eyes if not using cane slices)
- Standard playing card, or piece of card 9cm x 6cm
- 2 x 4mm black glass beads
- Sticky tape (eg sellotape)
- Two pairs of flat nosed pliers   • Wire cutters
- Knitting needle – I use 7mm diameter
- Polymer clay varnish. I use Darwi Vernis – optional
- Tissue blade
- Oven to cure clay in
- Tile to work on
- Sculpey Bake & Bond

CLAY:

These colours are for Lavender Bluebell.
As you can see I use a mixture of Premo and Fimo, but this is because I always buy large blocks of gold premo but prefer Fimo for canes.

- 1/2 x 56g (1oz) Premo Sculpey Accents Gold
- 85g (3oz) Fimo Professional True Magenta
- 85g (3oz) Fimo Professional Turquoise
- 113g (4oz) Fimo Professional White
- 44g (1.5oz) Fimo Professional Black
- Around 30g of scrap clay

23

Making the beak and feet:

Cut two pieces of wire, 10cm and 5cm, and join them together by twisting, leaving 2cm at the end for the beak.

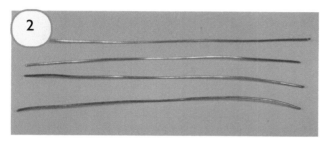

Cut four pieces of wire, each measuring 15cm. These are going to form the feet and legs.

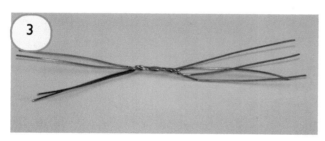

Using the two pairs of flat nosed pliers, start twisting the four pieces of wire together in the middle.

Continue twisting tightly but leave 2.5cm untwisted at each end.

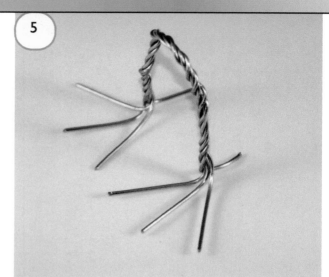

Bend the wire in the middle, then splay out the four untwisted bits of wire at each end. These are going to make the four toes; have three facing forward and one facing backwards. Finally trim the toes so the front ones are all the same length and the back one is slightly shorter.

Roll out some gold clay to a 21cm long log, 8mm diameter and cut the following:
6 x 3cm & 2 x 2cm for the feet
2 x 2cm for the beak
Round one end of all the pieces, following instructions on how to do this on page 21.

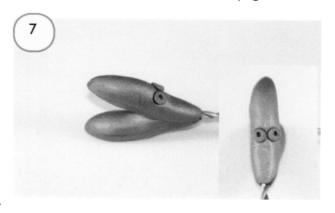

24

For the beak, take the two 2cm pieces of clay and push them, non-rounded end first, onto each prong of wire. Roll them together to join and taper at the joined end. To make the nostrils, roll small balls of clay and place them on the top, no further back than where the two gold pieces split. Make holes using a cocktail stick or needle tool.

To make the feet, push the longer pieces of clay on the front toes and the shorter pieces on the back toes.

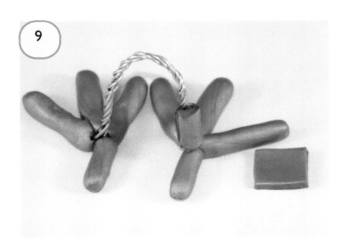

Roll some gold clay on PM1 and cut two 1.5cm x 1.5cm squares. Wrap these around the leg wire, just above the feet.

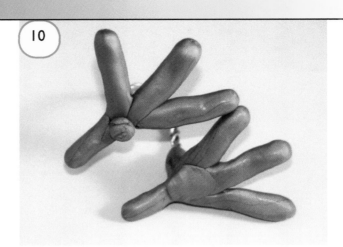

Make small balls of clay and put them underneath each foot, then smooth. This just fills in any gaps that may be there and makes a better base for the chicken to stand on.
Finally, using the knitting needle, spend some time smoothing out all the joins on the feet.

All joins smoothed out.

To make the claws, roll a 3mm diameter log of clay in the colour you want them to be, roll the end to a point and cut off 8mm. Make 8.

Using a thick knitting needle, I use 7mm diameter, make a hole in each toe. Take your claw and push it down into the hole, before gently easing it down to curve round the end of the toe. Try not to let the claws stick out as it makes them easy to break off.

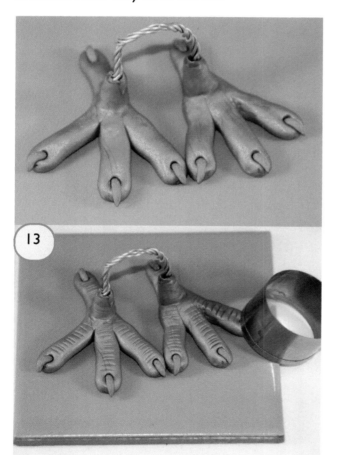

The final part of making the chicken feet is my favourite! Take a cutter, any one will do, or your tissue blade, and use the non sharp edge to make little marks up each toe, and round the leg. These do not have to be even, make them irregular. Your beak and feet are now ready to cure. Follow the clay manufacturers recommendation, but if using Fimo or Premo, cure them at 130° C for 30 minutes.

Making the body:

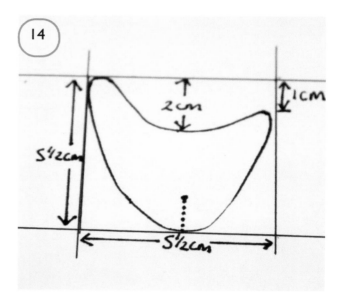

Cut a body shape in cardboard. To do this, first cut a 5.5cm square, then make the shape following the image above.

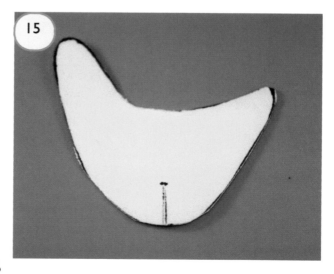

Take your chicken body shape and make a 1.2cm vertical cut from the middle of the base.

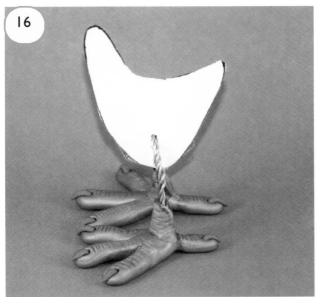

Slide your legs up to the top of the cut, making sure that the three longer toes are underneath the long, taller end of the cardboard shape, as this is the head end, and it's helpful if the chicken's feet are facing forward!

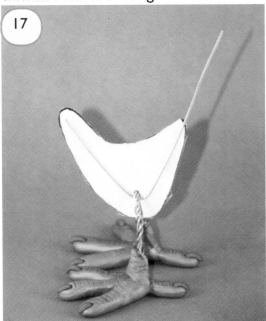

Cut a piece of wire 14cm long and tape it to the body, making the wire start from the head end, go underneath the leg wire, and out through the other pointed end of the cardboard shape.

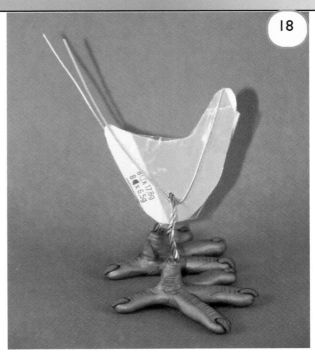

Repeat the other side.

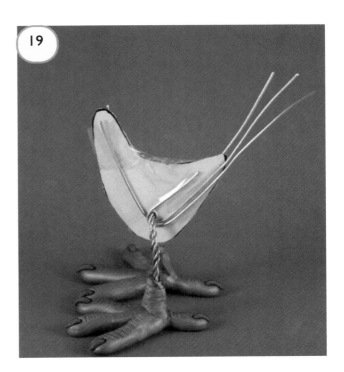

Cut a piece of wire 12cm long, wrap it round the leg wire on one side as shown, tape it and take out through the tail. You should now have three pieces of wire at the tail end.

27

20

Using the flat nosed pliers, twist the three tail wires together as shown. You can decide later what design and length of tail you want so don't cut them just yet.

21

Take your tin foil and tear or cut it into strips around 6cm wide. You will need 4-5 strips.

22

Take one strip of foil and wrap it round your chicken, making sure it covered the top half of the chicken completely.

23

Mould the tin foil to the shape of your chicken body.

Take another strip of tin foil and wrap it around the chicken, this time making sure that you cover the bottom half of the body, up to the top of the legs.

24

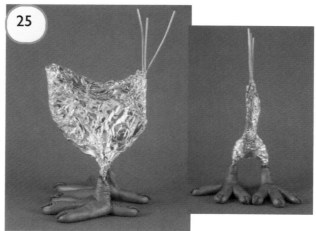

25

Again mould the foil to the body, making sure you have covered the wire up to the top of the legs.

28

Troubleshooting:

Listing to one side.

Leaning too far forward - your chicken will be unlikely to be able to stand without falling over.

Make sure your chicken isn't either leaning to one side, too far forward, or too far back.

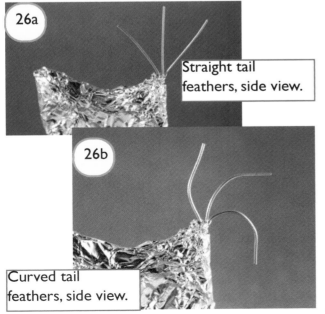

26a

Straight tail feathers, side view.

26b

Curved tail feathers, side view.

26c

Straight tail feathers, front view.

Decide what style of tail you want, look at the gallery at the end of the tutorial to see the different styles. The third photo, 26c, is the view from the head of the chicken, the tail fanning out from one side of the bird to the other. For Lavendar Bluebell I've chosen the style in the middle photo, 26b. Cut the wire to size, making sure that each wire is no longer than 3cm. Any longer and your chicken will fall backwards!

27

Take some scrap clay, roll on PM2 and cover your chicken, making sure that all the tin foil is covered. This doesn't have to be perfectly smooth as it will be covered by the feathers. If however you're making a chicken in a particular colour and adding slices of cane for decoration, then it will have to be smooth - see the spotty chicken in the gallery for an example of this.

The rear view of your covered chicken. Note the clay touches the top of the gold legs.

Making the first feather cane:

Stripy Bulls Eye:

Roll out some turquoise and white clay on PM0 and cut round a standard playing card (9cm x 6cm). Roll some black clay on PM7 and cut a piece 6cm x 3cm. Follow steps 1-2 on page 17, then the instructions on page 18, steps 1-4 to make a darker graduated Skinner blend.

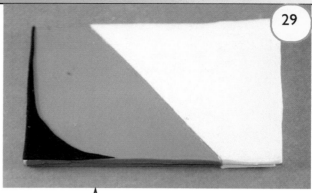

From this .. ⇑ ..... to this ⇓ ....

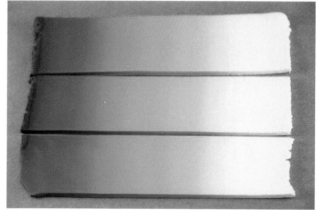

Cut your blend into three even width pieces.

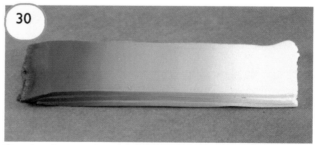

Stack the strips on top of each other, then pinch one end. This makes it easier to put through the pasta machine and prevents the three pieces from separating.

Roll the stack through the pasta machine on PM0, short end first, then PM2, and PM4, and finally PM6. Then roll up the cane following instructions on page 22, white end first. Cover the cane with a layer of white clay rolled on PM7, again following instructions on page 22.

Roll the Magenta clay on PM0 and cut three rectangles, 6cm x 3.5cm (or the width of your cane, see above).

Roll some black clay on PM4, lay each magenta rectangle on it and cut round.

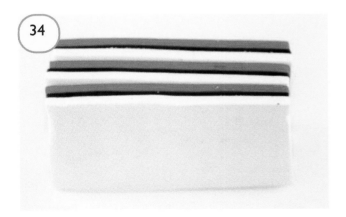

Roll some white clay on PM0, put each Magenta/black rectangle on it and cut round. You now have three rectangles, stack them on top of each other as shown.

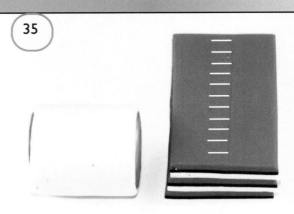

You're now going to make 5mm marks from the shorter edge. This is important as it is going to wrap round your cane so needs to be the right length.

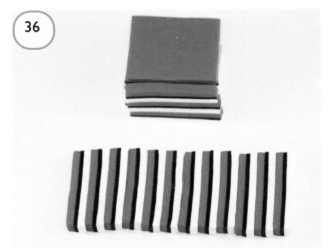

Cut five of the 5mm slices and lay them next to each other. Roll slightly with your clay roller to stick them together.

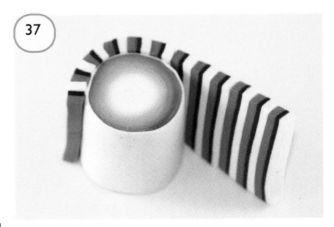

Wrap the stripy sheet round your cane. I find that five slices fits well round the cane, but if you need an additional one, or even just part of one, just cut it and add so that the whole cane is covered.

Finally wrap the cane in magenta clay, rolled on PM4, and your cane is completed.

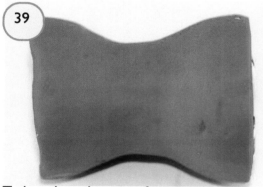

To lengthen the cane, first squeeze in the middle.

To lengthen the cane, first squeeze in the middle, then gently but firmly push the clay from the middle outwards, until your cane is the same diameter all the way along. You are aiming to push the clay out rather than pull it as this is less likely to distort the ends and you will lose less clay. Once you've done this you can roll it to lengthen.

Keep checking the ends, and trying to keep them as even as possible. As you see, I had some distortion, but not much, and there would have been a lot more wastage if I hadn't kept checking the ends and pushing and pulling the clay to keep it even.

Roll to 20cm, cut in half and cut off the distorted ends. Put the two remaining pieces of cane to one side to be used later. Feather cane number one is now completed.

Making the second feather cane:

Skinner Blend Jelly Roll:

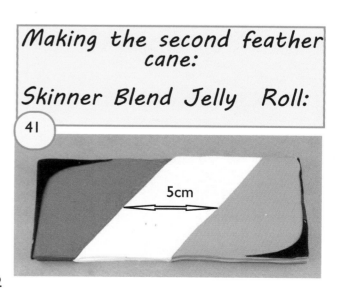

5cm

32

To make the blend for this cane, roll out the Magenta and Turquoise clay on PM0 and cut to the size of a standard playing card (9cm x 6cm). Follow steps 1 - 2 on page 17 but add a 5cm wide double thickness of white clay between the two colours as shown. Now you're going to follow steps 1-4 on page 18, but adding the black clay to both ends, on the Magenta as well as the Turquoise.

You end up with the above blend.

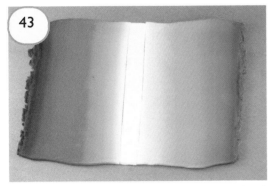

However, I want a wider amount of white, so I added a 2cm strip of white clay in the middle.

Cut the blend into two pieces.

Cut each piece into two, and stack, then pinch one end of each piece before putting them both through the pasta machine on PM0, short end first.

Roll some white clay on PM6, lay each strip on it and cut round. Then repeat with black clay, again on PM6.

Don't worry about covering with one long strip of thin clay, in this case black. It can be very tricky getting a long strip of thin clay and in certain circumstances, such as when the join isn't going to be seen, you can get away with covering it in sections. You can use several pieces, as long as the whole strip is covered, joins won't show as it is going to be rolled up.

Obviously the piece on the left has been trimmed and the piece on the right hasn't, I just left it like that to show you the two pieces.

You're now going to roll both the strips up. First pinch the turquoise end of one strip and the magenta end of the other, then roll each one up, pinched end first, with the black side on the outside.

Pinch the end just before you finish rolling it up, this will make a nicer end to the roll.

These are the two rolled canes. Now lengthen each of them until they measure 1.5cm diameter.

The finished canes, with a slice from each one. This Skinner blend jelly roll cane is one of my favourites, especially using both black and white to make the spiral.

Making the wings:

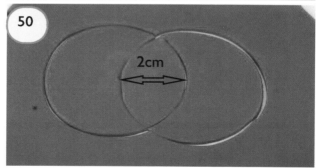

2cm

Roll some magenta clay on PM2 and using the 4cm circle cutter, cut two circles, overlapping by 2cm.

This will give you two identical shapes either side of the middle part which will be used to make the wings.

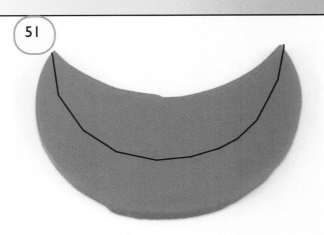

51

Make a mark in the clay from point to point, in a curve in the middle of the shape as shown.

Cut 2.5cm off the turquoise centred jelly roll cane and roll the cut off piece to 8mm diameter. Now flatten it slightly as shown in the picture on the right, and cut slices 1-2mm thick. You could cover the cane in glitter if preferred before flatterning and slicing, see page 21 for how to do this.

52

Take the cane slices and cut them so that they fit the lower half of the wing, making sure that the cut end is in the middle as this is going to be covered up later and laying them at an angle, pointing towards one end.

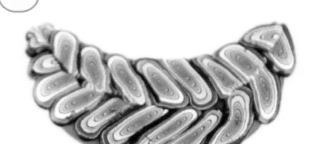

53

Now do the same on the top half, putting the slices on the top pointing to the same end to make it look like a leaf or feather.

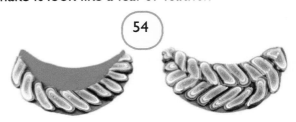

54

Cover the other wing the same way, but making sure that you make a mirror image of the first wing, in other words the cane slices are pointing in the opposite way. You need to do this so that when the wings are on your chicken, they both point backwards.

55

To make the centre part of your wing, take a 5mm slice from your stripy block, and put through the pasta machine, lengthways (stripes vertical) on PM0, then PM2 then PM4. Cut 2mm slices.

(56)

Place the strips end to end until you have a length that will reach from one wing tip to the other. Next roll some turquoise clay on PM4 and cut 1mm strips. Lay them either side of the stripy strip and roll gently to adhere.

(57)

Lay the stripy/blue strip in the middle of the wing as shown, pressing gently and cutting the ends off so they don't overhang.

(58)

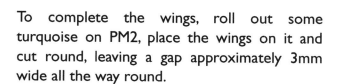

To complete the wings, roll out some turquoise on PM2, place the wings on it and cut round, leaving a gap approximately 3mm wide all the way round.

Now cure your wings following the clay manufacturer's recommended times, or if using Premo or Fimo cure for 30 minutes at 130°C.

Putting it all together:

(59)

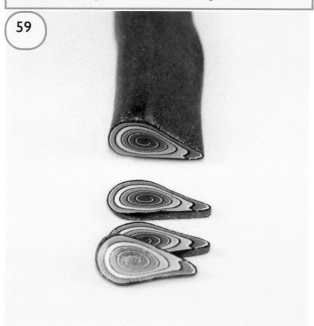

To make the feathers we're going to use cane 1, and the pink centred cane 2, shown above.

Cut cane 1 in half, and roll one half to 12mm diameter. Cut the pink centred cane in half and roll both halves to 12mm diameter. These are going to form your feathers.

Cover the canes in ultra fine glitter at this stage if you're using it, I covered cane 1 in a bright pink and cane 2 in turquoise. Once covered, press one edge of the cane to make a point then cut 2mm slices.

(60)

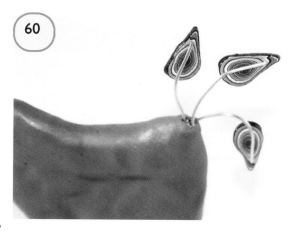

We're going to start with the tail, using slices from one of the second feather canes. Take three slices and start by putting one on the end of each of the tail wires, making sure that the wire goes almost to the end of the slice.

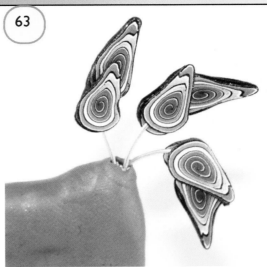

63

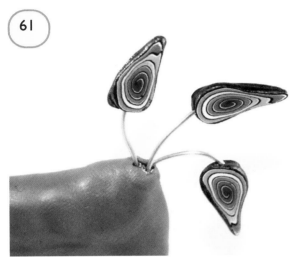

61

Take another three slices and place them on top of the first three, covering the wire. Press gently to join the two together.

As with the first slices, you're going to add the second slice over the first, capturing the wire and overlapping the above cane. You need to make sure no wire is showing.

Continue to cover the tail wires, it usually takes around three sets of slices, and finish with the middle one on the top, as shown in the following photographs.

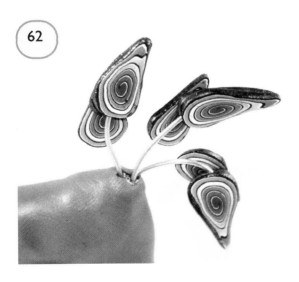

62

Place the next three slices underneath the first ones, overlapping as shown.

The view from the head end showing the cane slices overlapping.

64

Shape cane 1 as before and cut 2mm slices.

Continue to add layers of slices, overlapping the previous layer, and keeping the points facing the same direction. Try to place the slices in between the previous layer where possible.

67

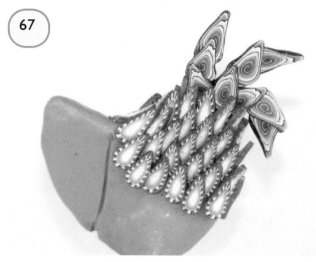

65

Place a layer of the cane 1 slices round the base of the tail feathers, points facing upwards.

Continue down the chicken, layering the feathers until you get near to the neck. Make a line round the neck where you want the different coloured feathers to be, and continue layering the slices up to the line.

68

66

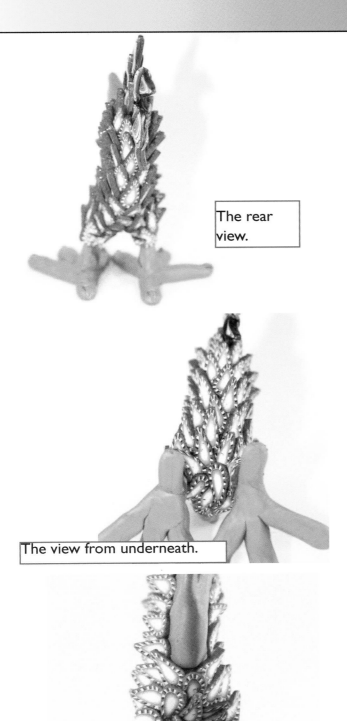

The rear view.

The view from underneath.

And finally the front view. Notice how the feathers go right up to the top of the gold legs, you need to cover the scrap clay completely.

Now with the same cane slices that you covered the tail wire with, continue layering the feathers towards the head.

70

Cover the whole of the neck and head area.

The front view. It doesn't matter if there is a bit of a gap at the top in the front as this is where the beak is going to be put, so it will be covered.

72

Take the beak and hold it up to the side of the chicken, with the beak part in the place that it will be inserted.

Now cut the wire at a place long enough to go well into the chicken, but not so it goes out the other side. I cut it around half the width of the chicken.

71

Put some Bake & Bond on the underside of each wing and place on the sides of the chicken. Put both on at the same time so you can push them on without touching the feathers.

Make sure they are at the same height, looking from the back and the front.

73

Take your needle tool and push it through the chicken at the point where the beak is going to be placed.

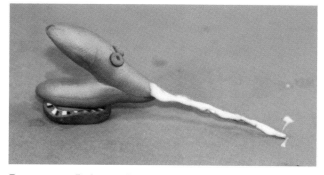

Put some Bake & Bond on the wire part of the beak.

40

To make the eyes, cut 2 x 3mm slices off the 15mm diameter stripy bulls eye cane. Alternatively you could cut 2 x 15mm circles in one colour, and 2 x 7mm in another colour, both on PM1.

Push the beak in, making sure that it's straight. It's easy to put it in and look at it from the side, then when you view your chicken from the front............. a wonky beak!   I've done it!

Put some Bake & Bond on the back of each eye and place either side of the head, finishing by pushing a 4mm black glass bead in the centre.

Next, holding the chicken by putting your finger and thumb on the eyes, make a cut in the top of the head and insert the three comb pieces. Finally push the cut together securing the comb.

Roll three pieces of clay around 1.5cm x 5mm each, with a rounded point at both ends. These are going to form the comb at the top of the head, you can make them whatever colour you like.

Cut 2 x 1.5cm diameter slices of the first cane, 3mm thick, and pull into teardrop shapes.

79

Put a little Bake & Bond on the two slices and place just under the beak, pointed end uppermost.

Your chicken is now ready to cure. All that's left to do now is make an egg for her.

Making the egg:

80

Roll some scrap clay on PMO and cut 4 x 3cm circles. Roll them all together into a ball, as shown on the left of the picture.

Take pieces of all the canes you've used, as well as any spare stripy cane, and cut thin slices off all. You want as wide a variety as possible.

81

Cover the ball of scrap clay with cane slices, making it as varied as possible.

Once covered, spend some time pushing all the cane edges together to make sure the scrap clay is completely hidden, then roll to make the ball smooth.

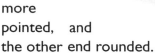

82

Roll the ball into the shape of an egg, making one end more pointed, and the other end rounded.

83

To cure both the chicken and the egg, place in a pre-heated oven at 130 ° C and cure for 30 minutes. I like putting them in cornflower to cure but it's not essential.

Once your chicken and egg have cured and cooled, you can varnish. This is not essential, but it really makes the chicken shine. Lavender Bluebell is now finished.

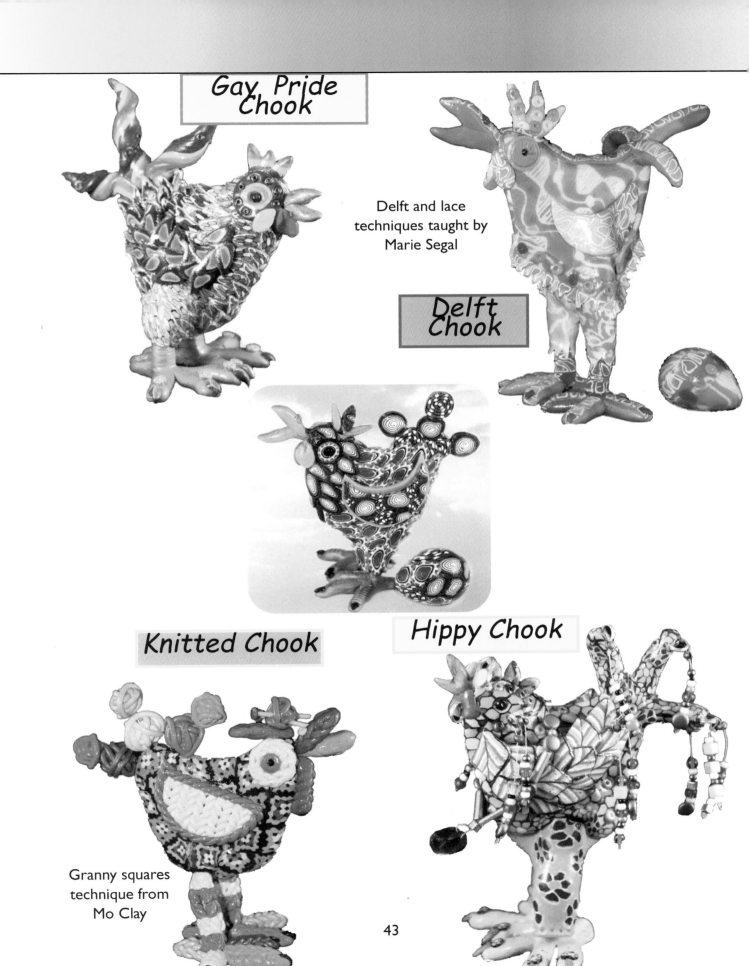

Gay Pride
Chook

Delft and lace
techniques taught by
Marie Segal

Delft
Chook

Knitted Chook

Hippy Chook

Granny squares
technique from
Mo Clay

43

Scottish
Chooks

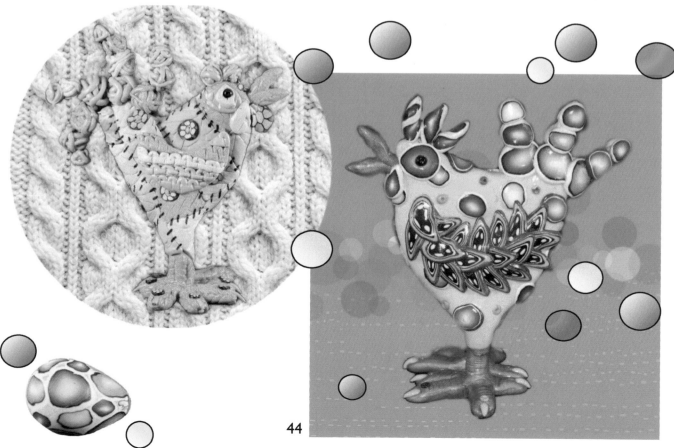

44

TOOLS & MATERIALS:

- Pasta machine
- Tissue blade
- Acrylic or metal clay roller
- Needle tool / cocktail stick
- Tile to work on
- Oven to cure clay in
- Good quality tin foil
- 4 x 22cm of 1mm wire – I get it from the garden centre or DIY store
- A ball tool approx. 13mm diameter
- Circle cutters 3cm diameter (and 1cm & 5mm for the eyes if not using cane slices)
- Oval cutters 1.5cm and 1.2cm – you can make these by hand or use circle cutters so they're not essential
- 2 x 4mm black glass beads
- Sticky tape (eg sellotape)
- Two pairs of flat nosed pliers
- Knitting needles – I use 7mm diameter and 4mm diameter ones
- Sculpey Bake & Bond

CLAY:

These colours are for the orange Sophie pony shown.
- 1 x 56g Premo Sculpey Orange
- 2 x 56g Premo Sculpey Accents Pearl
- 1/2 x 56g Premo Sculpey Accents Bronze
- 1/4 x 56g Premo Sculpey Black
- A small amount of Premo Sculpey Accents Silver (about the size of a walnut)

Sophie the Pony:

I have been riding or driving ponies since the age of three, so of course a pony just had to be made! Our family has had many ponies over the years, but around the time I designed the ponies we lost a lovely little mare called Sophie. She was a chestnut Welsh pony and had the sweetest temperament, so this pony is therefore named Sophie in her memory.

Sophie had a friend, Blue. Blue and Sophie were the lead two ponies in my team, and were the best. Blue was a typical male and liked to snatch some grass whenever possible, even in the competition at times; therefore I have made Blue with some grass in his mouth! He was, and still is, my very favourite pony. He is 29 now and retired, but lives with the other ponies, ruling the roost happily, and is very much loved.

Sophie

Blue

45

Making the body:

The above picture shows the steps taken to make the foil body. Start by taking a piece of foil 20cm x 15cm and rolling it loosely into a ball.

Gradually press all around the ball, keeping the round shape but beginning to flatten two sides, like a fat coin.

Continue compressing it, I like to use my clay roller to tap it into shape and roll it along the work surface to get an smooth edge. You are aiming to make it into a kidney bean shape.
Finally roll the sides of the edge along the work surface to round them, and make an indentation in the top of the shape - this will be the top of Sophie's back.

Using a needle tool or cocktail stick, make two holes all the way through the shape, positioned 2cm apart, 0.8cm from the bottom edge. After using the cocktail stick, make the holes slightly larger by pushing through a 4mm diameter tool like a knitting needle. This will make it easier to push the wire through.

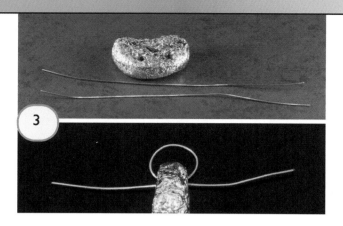

Take one of the 22cm pieces of wire and push it through one of the holes, then loop it round and push it through the same hole again as shown. Using two pairs of pliers, pull the wire fairly tight, making sure the two ends are roughly the same length.

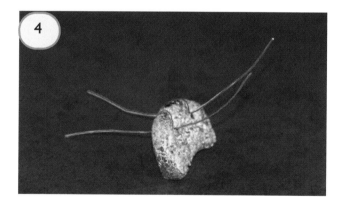

Repeat with the second piece of wire in the other hole. I've highlighted the two wires in red and blue to make it easier to see how they look when finished. Your wire will be silver!

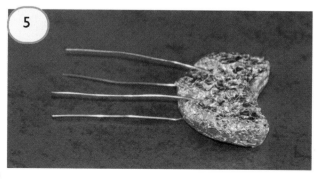

46

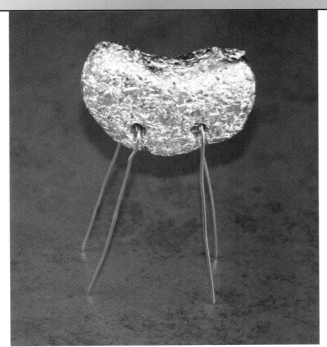

Straighten the legs and trim them so they are all the same length.

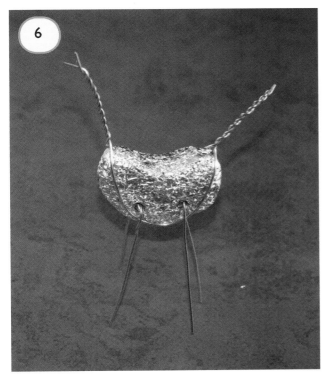

Take the third piece of wire and position it on the body as shown, leaving approximately 9cm for the head and neck, taking the wire underneath the two leg wires, and out at the opposite end for the tail. Use tape to secure it

to the foil, then repeat with the last piece of wire on the other side, and again secure with tape.

Once both wires are in place, take a pair of pliers and twist the two head pieces of wire together, then the two tail pieces.

Don't trim them at this point as you won't know how long you need them until later.

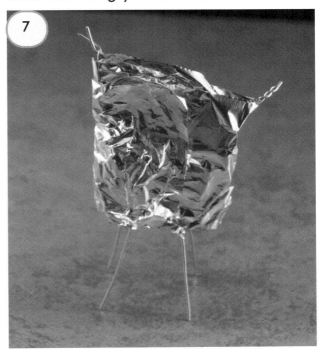

Take a piece of tin foil, approx 30cm x 5cm. Wrap it round the pony body as shown, making sure there is a little overhang above and below the pony. Gently mould the foil to the body, securing the top of the legs and

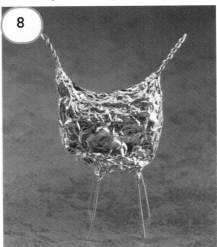

making sure it is all covered. It is important to leave the tail without foil.

Making the hooves:

Roll some black clay to PM0 and cut 4 x 3cm circles. Roll each circle into a ball, then, keeping the ball on the table, twist it round to make a flatter base. You are looking for a cone shape with a flat bottom. Lastly roll out a thin log of silver clay, this will make the horseshoes.

Cut the silver log at an angle and place on the flattened base of the black dome. Gently press the silver log round the edge of the hoof, then cutting off, again at an angle, leaving a small gap as shown.

Gently flatten the silver part, then make two ridges as shown in the third picture from the left. Lastly make some holes in the ridges to imitate horseshoe nails. Put the hooves to one side for later.

Making the Spots:

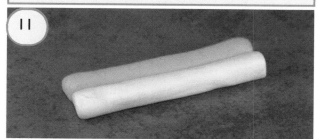

Roll the orange and pearl clay on PM0 and cut 3 x 3cm circles of each colour. Roll each colour into a ball, and then a log around 7cm long. Place side by side as shown. Now follow the Mo Clay method of making a blend on page 20, steps 1 - 8.

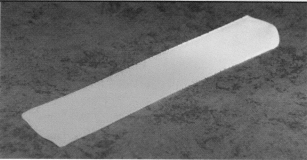

You will end up with a long piece of graduated clay. Set the pasta machine to PM2 and put the long piece of clay through again, then again on PM4. You will end up with a longer and thinner piece of blended clay.

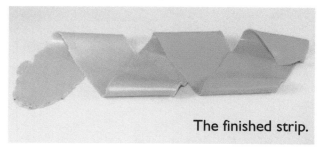

The finished strip.

Roll up the clay, starting from the orange end, using the Carol Simmons technique on page 22.

Roll out some bronze clay on PM4 and cover the cane, following the technique shown on page 22.

Lengthen the cane until it measures approximately 1cm diameter and cut in half. You now have two small canes.

48

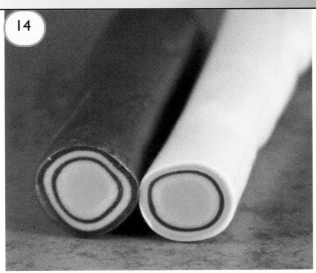

14

For the cane on the left, cover with a layer of pearl on PM3, then bronze on PM4. For the cane on the right cover with a layer of orange on PM3, then pearl on PM4.

You now have two slightly different bulls eye canes. Of course, you can make any colour or combination of colours and widths of layers, possibly having a pearl to bronze blend in the middle instead of orange. I have just shown you a basic cane for the spots.

Making the legs:

15

With the pasta machine on PM0 cut out 5 x 3cm circles of orange clay and 5 x 3cm circles of pearl clay. Follow the Mo Clay steps 1 to 8 on page 20 to make a blend. Once you have the clay blended, cut it into four equal parts as shown.

16

You are going to roll each section into a log, but before you do, take your tissue blade and make a cut at an angle from 3mm to the edge one side, as shown below:

Making a bevelled edge helps the end of the strip of clay blend into the main cane. Because the clay includes pearl clay, which has mica particles, it is difficult to get a join without it showing, and making the edge thinner, the join is far less noticable.

Now roll up each section into a log, rolling the edge that doesn't have the angled edge first, then roll into a cone shape by holding (if you're right handed) your right hand first finger against the pearl end, and rolling the log with your left hand at an angle (little finger lower than your ring finger) and rolling towards your right hand. This should keep the cane the same length but make it into a cone shape.

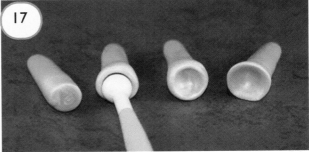

17

To finish the end, take a ball tool roughly 13mm diameter and twist it in the pearl end of the leg until you have a round hole. Finally, with your finger and thumb pinch all round the edges of the hole, making it thinner and slightly wider.

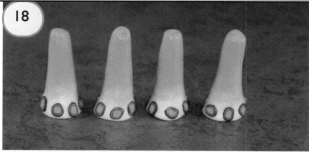

Cut a 2cm piece off one of the spot canes and roll to around 5mm diameter. Cut 7 thin slices of cane for each leg and place around the bottom of each, trying to make them as evenly spaced as possible. If you want to smooth them down and blend them into the leg, take a large knitting needle and gentle roll it over the edges of the cane slices. Put the legs to one side to add to the body later.

Covering the body:

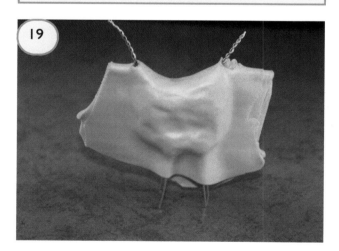

Mix orange and pearl, the equivalent of half a 56g block, in the ratio of 1 part orange to 3 part pearl:

1/8 of a block of orange &
3/8 of a block of pearl

Put through the pasta machine on PM1 and lay it over the pony's body, making sure it covers both sides as shown.

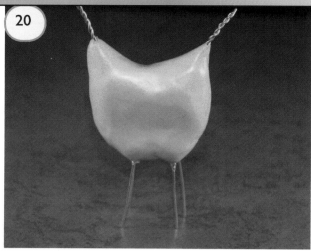

Cut the excess clay all round the body then smooth all over; I like to use a large knitting needle for this, rolling it rather than dragging it over all the joins. Spend some time doing this, making the body smooth all over. If there are any parts that are uneven or have dents, you can add more clay and smooth it in.

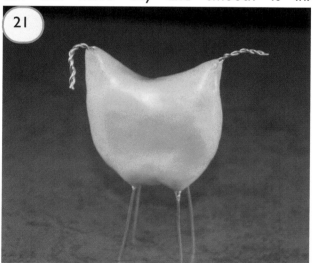

At this point you bend the wire to the position you want it to be finally. I have decided to have Sophie's tail flowing out behind her and her head looking to the left.
You can also trim the wires to the required length. However, be careful not to cut either of them too short - as I have done with Sophie's head!! Around 6cm would have been an ideal length for her head and neck. Finally cover the tail with a thin layer of clay, the same colour as the body.

The head and neck:

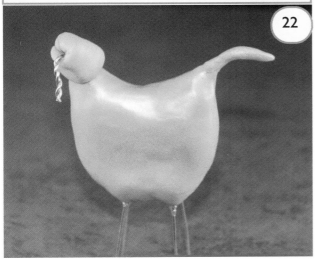

Using the same clay as for the body, roll it out on PM0 and cut 2 x 3cm circles. Roll the two clay circles together into a rectangle and wrap this round the neck wire.

Join the neck to the body, smoothing all the joins.

To make the head, cut three 3cm circles on PM0 one in orange, one in pearl, and one the

colour of the body.
Roll each one into a log and place them together with the pearl in the middle. Make a Mo Clay blend following steps 1 to 8 on page 20.

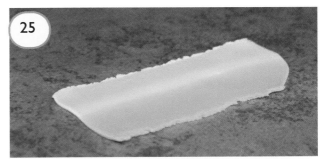

Before rolling the blended sheet into a log, cut along one edge at an angle, the same way you did in step 16. This will help the seam blend in.

Roll into a log then mould it into a cone shape as shown above; I have made the darker end the muzzle so that the head blends onto the neck with the same colour.

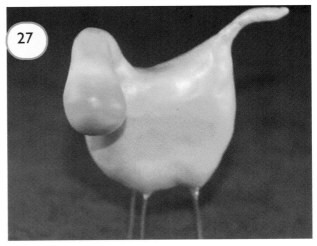

Attach the head to the neck, smoothing out the joins.

Making the ears:

Roll out some bronze clay on PM2 and cut 2 x 1.5cm ovals. Roll out some pearl clay on PM2 and cut out 2 x 1.2cm ovals. Make a point at each end of the four ovals then place the pearl ovals on the bronze ovals, matching up the bottom ends.

Finish by using a narrow knitting needle to make a mark along 3/4 of the ear and pinch the base as shown. I like to cure the ears for 25 minutes at 130 °C which makes them easier to add to the head, but this is optional. You could also make ears in different combinations of colours.

Attaching the legs and hooves:

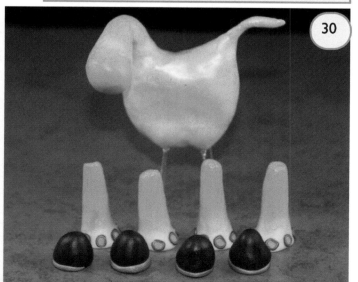

First cut the leg wires down to 5mm longer than the legs.

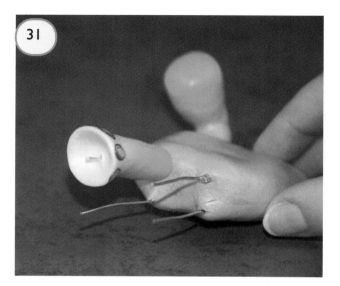

Carefully thread the wire through the leg so that it comes out in the middle. If it comes out elsewhere, just pull it back and re-do it. I rarely get all four perfect first time and you won't see the holes.

Next push the hoof on, making sure that the gap in the horse shoe is facing towards the back of the pony.

52

Repeat with all four legs and hooves.

Using a large knitting needle, smooth the joins between the legs and the body and stand the pony on a firm surface, such as a tile, ensuring that the legs are all of equal length and the pony stands securely.

Do not push down more than very gently as this will flatten the horse shoes.

If, once you have put the hooves on you find that the wire is sticking out of the bottom, use the wire cutters to cut it off.

Making the face:

Roll two small balls of bronze clay and place on the muzzle where the nostrils would be.

I learnt this technique from Birdy Heywood when making dragon nostrils.

Make the nostril holes by putting a knitting needle in at the bottom of the ball, and keeping the point in place, move the needle in a circular motion up towards the top of the ball.

It might be a good idea to practice this on a scrap ball of clay first.

The eyes can either be made from a 1cm diameter slice of a spot cane, or you could cut circles of clay 1cm and 5mm diameter instead to make the eyes. Put a 4mm black glass bead in the middle of each eye and push in firmly.

Above each eye make a hole using a 4mm knitting needle and put in a little Bake & Bond. Insert the ears.

As I said earlier, it is much easier to put the ears in if they've been cured first as they don't get distorted, but it is possible to put them in without being cured; I've done it many times when I've got to the ear stage and realised I've forgotten to cure them!

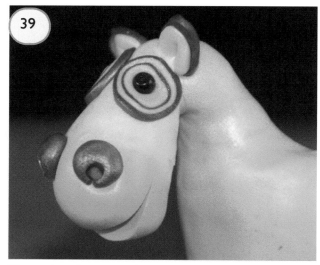

To make the mouth, use your tissue blade to make a cut, then carefully press at each corner inwards, which will make it slightly open.

Putting on the spots:

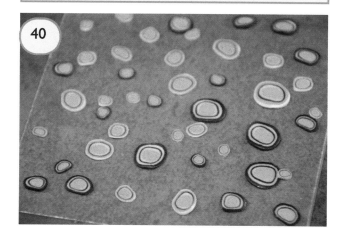

Cut thin slices from both spot canes in differing sizes.

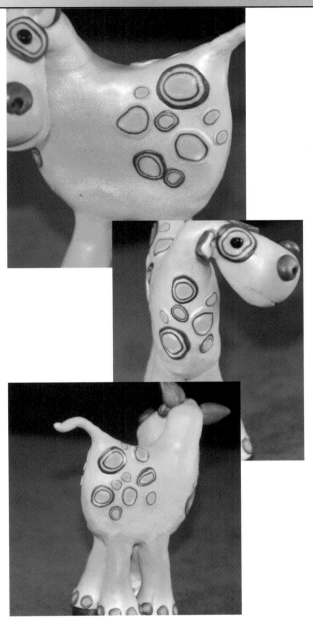

Take the scraps of clay from the canes, as well as small amounts of the orange, pearl and bronze clay. Roll them out into little logs, 3mm in diameter.

For the mane:
Make around 14 logs, 2cm long, and pointed at one end.

For the tail:
Make around 14 logs, at whatever length you have made the tail, pointed at both ends. Also make 6 or 7 x 2cm logs, also pointed at both ends.

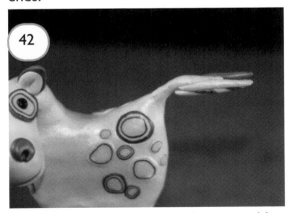

42

First make the tail. Take a tail piece and lay it on the tail, starting at the base of the tail where it meets the pony's bottom. Continue laying the logs all the way round until the covering clay is hidden by the logs.

Place them on the pony in a random pattern; I have put them on both her hind quarters and her chest. It's a good idea to put them on very lightly to see what they look like before fixing them more securely by either pressing on them, or using a knitting needle to smooth down the edges of the spots.

It's better to put too few spots on rather than too many as you can always add more at a later date, but once they're securely on, they won't come off without leaving a mark.

55

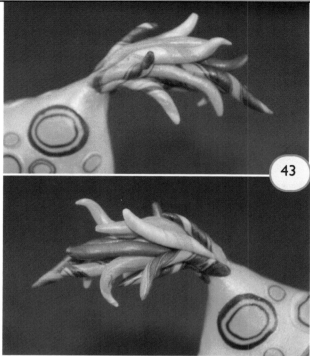

43

Once you've covered the tail with one layer of logs, put in some shorter 2cm logs so the tail looks fuller, then carefully manipulate the logs to make the tail have movement. This is one of my favourite parts.

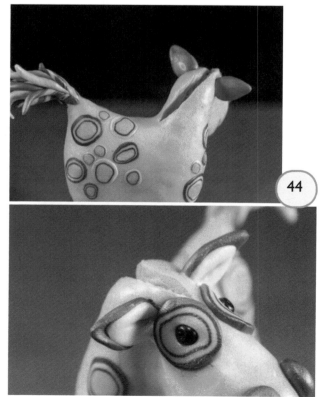

44

With your tissue blade, or a craft knife if you prefer, make a deep slit from the top of the eyes, along the neck to the base of the neck.

Put a line of Bake & Bond along the bottom of the whole cut.

45

Starting from the head end, take one of the mane pieces and place, square end first, into the cut.

Push it up as tight to the end of the cut you can, then put in another one, making sure that each log is well down into the cut, and pushed tight against the one in front.

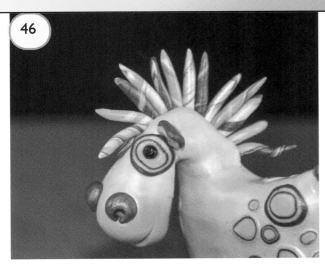

46

Keep placing the mane logs in until you reach the end. While you are putting them in, do not bend them over at all, leave them looking like she has a Mohican hair style for now. Once all are in, gently but firmly push the cut closed, securing the logs inside with the Bake & Bond.

47

Finally arrange the mane as you like. This can make a real difference to the pony's character so spend some time playing with it, looking from both sides to see what it looks like. She is now complete. All that's left to do is to cure her.

Preheat the oven to 130°C and cure for 30 minutes. Leave to cool completely before varnishing. I use Darwi Vernis gloss varnish because I like my ponies shiny, but varnishing is totally optional.

Lollipop Pony

Singing in the rain!

It always takes a few attempts before I get to the finished design. This was my first pony; as you can see it is a little like something that was around in the dinosaur age! However, there were many things I liked about it, and it gave me something to work from.

I made this little pony for my mother as she loves flowers. She named her Ermintrude. I'm sure that was a cow?!! but she did have a flower in her mouth so I see the connection. Ermintrude lives happily among the antiques at Brickwall Farm.

58

Ollie the Owl and his Parliament:

- Pasta machine
- Tissue blade
- Rigid blade
- Acrylic or metal clay roller
- Needle tool / cocktail stick
- Tile to work on
- Tile approx 10cm x 10cm
- Oven to cure clay in
- A standard playing card. or card 9cm x 6cm
- A round light bulb
- A toilet roll. cut in half lengthways
- 60cm x 30cm tin foil
- Ultra fine glitter. I used silver and green – optional
- Circle cutters. diameter 4cm. 3cm. 12mm. 5mm
- Heart cutter 2.5cm or....
- Teardrop cutter 2.5cm for the wings. Use either heart or teardrop for each owl
- 6 x 4mm black glass beads
- Sculpey Bake & Bond
- Polymer clay varnish. I use Darwi Vernis – optional

CLAY:

- 1 x 56g Premo Sculpey Accents Bright Green Pearl
- 1 x 56g Premo Sculpey Accents Peacock Pearl
- 1 x 56g Premo Sculpey Accents 18k Gold
- 1 x 56g Premo Sculpey White
- 1 x 56g Premo Sculpey Gold
- 1/2 x 56g (28g) Premo Sculpey Black
- Approximately 100g scrap clay

Oh these owls!

They have gone through so many changes since I started making them that this is the second time I've taken photos of the stages, and even now I do some things slightly differently. Just about every friend and family member has an owl or two, partly because I'm running out of space in the house - they're very addictive to make!

Making the owl bodies:

Take a 30cm x 20cm piece of tin foil and roll it loosely into a log shape. Then gradually squeeze it down until it is a log measuring approximately 4.5cm high. For a shorter owl make it 4cm, taller owl 5cm. Roll the log on a smooth surface to remove lumps.

Condition some scrap clay and roll it out on the second thickest setting of the pasta machine. Place the foil log on the clay and first cut a straight line behind the log, then two lines 1cm wider than the log each side as shown. Roll the clay round the log, cut to size, and fold the extra clay round each end to cover.

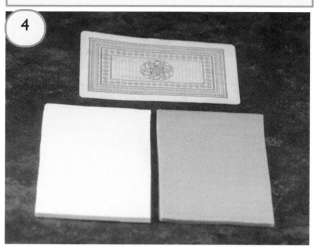

Make three and put to one side.

Making the canes – start with two Skinner blends

Roll out some white clay and some gold clay on PM0 and cut each colour to the size of a playing card (9cm x 6cm). Now follow the instructions on page 17 to make your gold/white blend.

The finished blend.

Make a second Skinner blend with the peacock pearl and the bright green pearl, again rolling on PM0. However, this time you're going to add a 1.5cm strip of white clay (double thickness) in between the two colours as shown.

Then roll slightly and make into a blend as you did the white and gold.

60

Making the leaf cane:

6

First cut the peacock and green blend in half lengthways as shown.

Put each half separately through the pasta machine on PM2 lengthways (either the green or peacock end first), then place one on top of the other and pinch one of the short ends before putting the double thickness of clay through again on PM1. Now put the pasta machine onto PM3 and put the strip through, again, then finally on PM5. You should now have a long strip of clay.

7

Follow the steps on page 22 to roll into a cane, green end first. Gently roll it so it gets fatter and shorter, rolling with your hands moving towards each other, as opposed to the usual way of rolling which makes the clay grow longer and thinner. Continue until you have a shorter, thicker log, 3cm high.

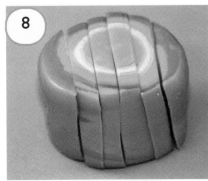

8

With your tissue blade make 5 evenly spaced cuts through the cane, although it's a leaf cane, so uneven is also fine.

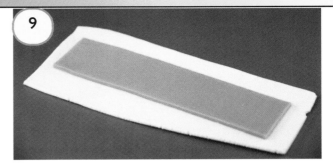

9

Roll some gold clay on PM1 and cut a piece 3cm x 13cm. Roll out some white clay to the same thickness, lay the gold on it and cut round. Gently pinch one of the short sides of the gold/clay strip and put it through the pasta machine at PM0, short side first. * Cut a 4cm piece and put to one side for later, then put the remaining long strip through the pasta machine on PM1 and finally PM3.

> *Alternative technique:
> You could fold the strip in half at this stage, deciding whether you want the gold or the white in the middle, and put through the pasta machine on PM0. Cut a 4cm piece off and put to one side, and put the remaining strip through the pasta machine on PM1, and finally PM3.

You will now have a long strip which will be used to make the leaf veins.

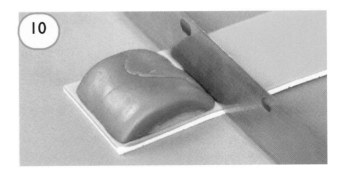

10

Take one of the pieces of the cane and place it on the strip as shown. Cut round the slice of cane trimming the gold/white clay to size.

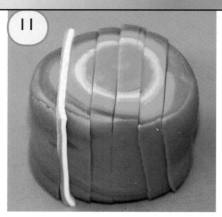

Put the covered slice back into the cane then repeat with the remaining four pieces of cane.

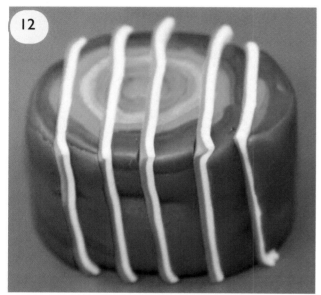

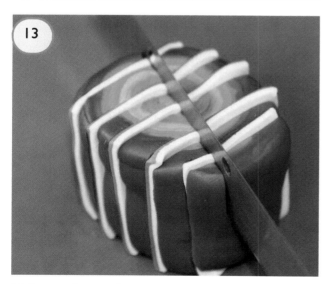

Make a diagonal cut through the slices, then take the 4cm piece of gold/white clay cut off earlier and lay it on one side of the leaf.

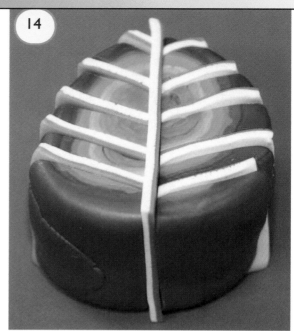

Turn the remaining half of the leaf round and put it back, this gives you the leaf vein effect.

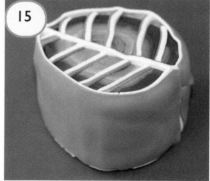

Wrap the remaining peice of clay you used for the veins round the cane, and your leaf cane is ready to reduce.

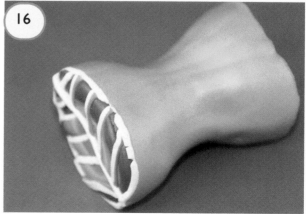

Start by squeezing the cane in the middle.

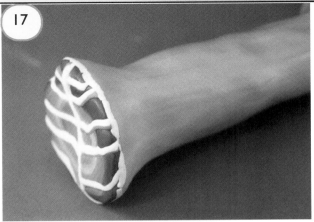

17

Then gently but firmly 'push' the clay from the middle towards the ends of the cane. You are not pulling the cane to make it smaller and longer, you are pushing the clay out which makes it less likely that you will lose so much clay at each end. Keep looking at the ends, and if they are becoming distorted, push them back into shape.

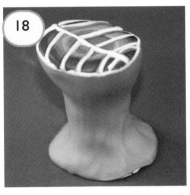

18

I sometimes press one end onto the work surface to help it remain flat and reduce distortion as I'm lengthening the cane. Continue reducing until the cane measures 1.5cm in diameter.

Chop off the distorted ends until you have a clear leaf pattern, and your first cane is complete. The cane slice on the left is cut from the cane when it is in a log shape, and the slice on the right is cut from the cane once it's been shaped into a leaf.

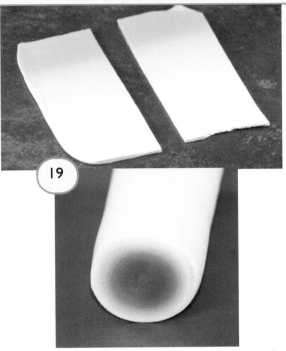

19

Take the gold/white blend and cut in half lengthways. Follow the same process as you did for the peacock green blend, and roll up with the gold inside. Roll the clay into a 6cm long log.

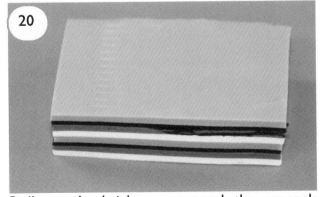

20

Roll out the bright green pearl, the peacock pearl and the white on PM1 and cut 2 peices of each colour, 6cm x 4cm. Roll out some black clay on the PM4, and cut 2 peices, 6cm x 4cm. Stack the rectangles in the following order: white, peacock, black, green, then repeat this pattern. Straighten one of the 6cm edges by cutting a thin slice off with your tissue blade.

63

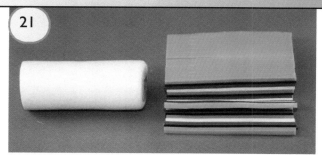

Starting from the straightened edge, make marks 3mm apart. You can see that the width of the stripy stack is the same as the length of the cane. I use a Marxit tool to make the 3mm marks, but I like gadgets!

With a rigid blade, cut five 3mm slices, then lay them on the work surface next to each other. Roll them gently with your roller to help them stick together, then place them carefully round the cane. This should be enough to cover the cane, but if needed, cut another slice.

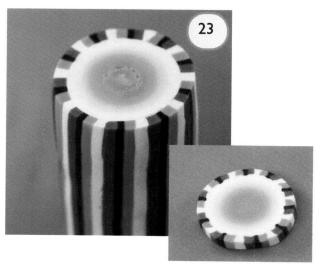

The stripy bulls eye cane is complete. Cut the cane in half and roll one half to 1.5cm diameter.

Making the watercolour cane:

I call this my watercolour cane because I was experimenting with stripes of clay on a peice of black clay, and the resulting cane looked like it had been painted in watercolour.

Start by rolling out 3mm diameter logs of the peacock, gold, white and green clay. Cut 4 sections 8cm long of each of the four colours, making 16 x 8cm rolls. Place the rolls next to each other in the following repeated pattern - peacock, gold, white, green.

Flatten the sheet slightly with your clay roller to help the rolls adhere to each other, and put through the pasta machine on PM1, <u>with the stripes running down vertically</u>.

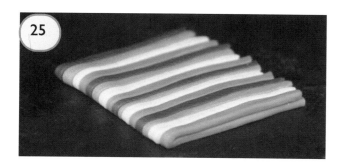

Fold the clay in half, top to bottom, lining up the colours, and put through the pasta machine again, folded side first. Repeat until the stripes are slightly blurred.

This is how it looks once the colours are slightly blurred. Cut off a piece 1cm wide from the less straight edge. This will be used later for a stomach.

The completed watercolour cane.

26

Roll some black clay on PM3 and lay the stripy sheet on top, cutting to shape.

My sister Ruth's owl, showing that every slice is different if you role the cane up the other way. It makes an eclectic and colourful owl.

27

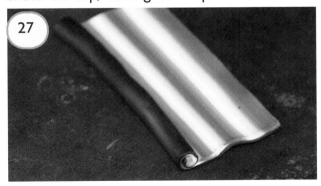

Put the black lined sheet through the pasta machine on PM1 (making sure you are putting it through with the stripes going down so they don't get wider), then roll up, rolling from the LONG side as shown.

Your watercolour cane is now completed. Roll to 1.5cm diameter.

The three completed canes:

Making the owl stomachs:

Now it's time to make the parts of the owls that are going to be cured first. To make each stomach roll out scrap clay on PM1 and cut a 4cm circle. Roll the clay into a ball, then put it on the work surface and shape it into a dome around 3.5cm in diameter. Make three of these.

Stomach 1: Blended Spotty

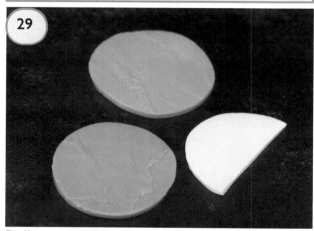

Roll some gold, green and white clay on PM1 and cut a 4cm circle of gold and green, and half a 4cm circle in white. Roll each colour into a log, 6cm long, and place side by side with the white in the middle.

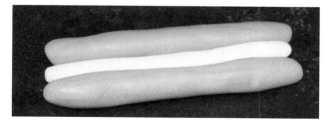

Follow the Mo Clay method of making a blend on page 20.

Once you have made the blend, put it through the pasta machine on PM2 without folding in order to make it thinner. Make sure you put it through lengthways, you don't want the stripes wider. Now take the 4cm circle cutter and cut a circle of the blend, making sure some of each of the colours are showing.

Carefully lay the blended clay circle over your scrap clay dome, smoothing out any air bubbles, then wrap the spare clay round the edge of the dome, pulling it round as shown so that the edges of the dome do not show any scrap clay.

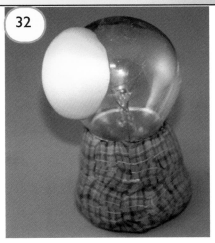

This is where the light bulb comes into play.

Place your stomach onto the bulb, where you can decorate it further without distorting the shape. It also helps make a nicer dome shape on the stomach.

You will notice that I've put clay round the base of the lightbulb so it stands on its own. If you don't want to do this, a cardboard toilet paper roll cut to size works well to hold the light bulb upright.

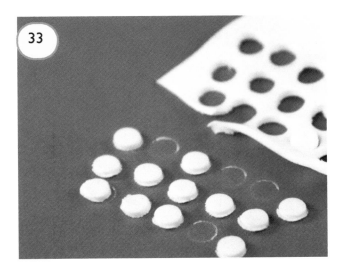

Roll out some white on PM4 and cut out some 5mm circles. Even with good Kemper cutters, as you can see they can leave a 'furry' edge. Take a bit of time to roll the edges of the circles between your thumb and first finger to smooth them out. It's little details like this that make a huge difference to the finished project.

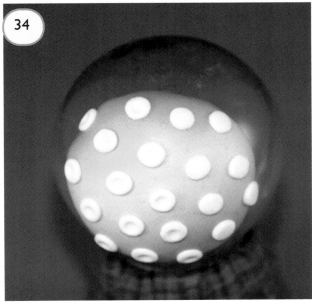

Place the circles on the stomach in whatever pattern you like. I then use a ball tool to make an indentation in each circle.

As you can see, you can use any shape cutter. In the above picture I've used a petal shape to make little flowers, with a small ball of peacock clay in the middle.

67

Stomach 2: Stripy

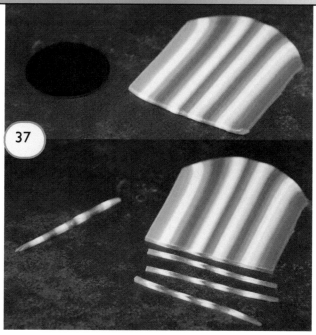

For the stripy stomach, take two slices from the stripy block you made for the second cane, put them together as you did in step 22, roll to join, then put them lengthways through the pasta machine on first PM0 then PM2. Cut a 4cm circle.

Take the peice of stripy clay that you cut off from the sheet you made for the watercolour cane, and cut three thin strips.

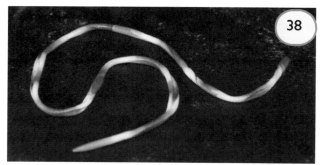

Cover a scrap clay dome as before in step 31, then put on the light bulb. If you like you can use the ball tool to make additional decoration on it.

Join the three strips together to make one long one, roll it a little all the way along - it doesn't have to be even - and make one end pointed.

Stomach 3: Spiral

First roll out some black clay on PM3 and cut a 4cm circle. Use this to cover the third scrap clay dome.

Place the pointed end in the middle of the black dome, winding it round in an increasing circle until you reach the outer edge.

Press down gently to adhere. I've made one with a white background to show you the difference. Again I've used a ball tool to make little indentations, but this is entirely optional. Place the third stomach on the light bulb with the other two.

The Owl Eyes:

I'm going to show you several different ways to make eyes, you just need to choose which ones you like. You will need three pairs of eyes for your three owls.

For these eyes, cut two 3mm slices from the stripy bulls eye cane, 2cm in diameter. Place a 4mm black glass bead in the middle of each eye.

Put the eyes onto the light bulb, bead side down. This creates a nice shape for the eye. As you can see, the bead has broken through the clay. That's fine, just put little balls of clay over the top. This side won't show so it doesn't have to look pretty.

These eyes are made in exactly the same way, but using slices of the watercolour cane. They also go on the light bulb to cure.

To make eyes with eyebrows, roll a peice of leaf cane to 1.5cm diameter and cut two 3mm slices off it. Mould them into a leaf shape and put them over the top of the two eyes. These eyes can be cured on the light bulb, but they also look nice cured flat on a tile.

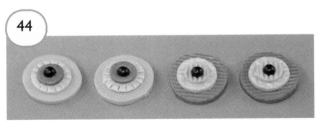

These eyes are made from three different size circles: 2cm, 12mm & 8mm.

Roll one coloured clay on PM2 and cut 2 x 2cm circles. Roll the other two colours on PM4 and cut the 12mm and 8mm circles.

Stack the three circles as shown. I like to texture some of the circles; you could use dots, lines, or you could also experiment with the stripy clay as one of the circles. Finally put in the glass bead and cure on a tile

45

These eyes are made with 2cm diameter stripy bulls eye canes, then an eyebrow of peacock clay.

To make the eyebrows the same size, roll out the clay on PM2 and using a 2cm circle cutter, cut two circles, overlapping each other. The two peices either side of the centre peice will be identical.

Place these on the top part of each eye and make small balls in gold and green to line the underside. Make a small hole in each ball with a cocktail stick or ball tool. Add the glass beads and cure the eyes flat on a tile.

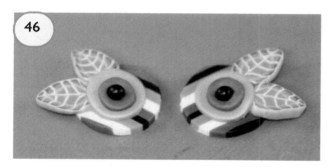

46

These eyes are made from 2cm diameter circles of stripy clay, with 1.5cm gold circles and 8mm peacock circles. In between the largest and medium size circles are tucked two leaf cane slices. These are best cured on the light bulb, but can be cured flat on a tile.

Covering a cane in glitter:

For the last eye design, I like to cover a piece of leaf cane in ultra fine glitter. When cut, it makes the edges of each slice sparkle. Polymer clay artist Birdy Heywood showed me how to do this, and I very rarely make an owl without glitter somewhere.

Follow the instructions on page 21 to cover the leaf cane with ultra fine glitter. For the last eye design you need to reduce a piece of the leaf cane to 8mm in diameter before covering with glitter. Covering in glitter is totally optional.

47

Roll some gold clay on PM2 and cut 2 x 12mm circles and 2 x 6mm circles.

Cut a thin slice off each end of the leaf cane, then pinch each end at the top of the leaf. Next pinch along the cane between the two end pinches; this makes the pointed part at the top of the leaf. Do the same slightly at the bottom, then cut 16 slices. Arrange them on the circle as shown.

70

Place the 6mm circles in the middle and push a 4mm black glass bead in each one.

If you prefer plainer ears, take some clay and mould into ear shapes, making sure the bottom part is longer to push into the head. You can make leaf-like marks on them, texture them, or leave them plain.

Finally place carefully, face down on the light bulb. You can see what they look like by looking through the other side of the bulb.

The Owl Ears:

48

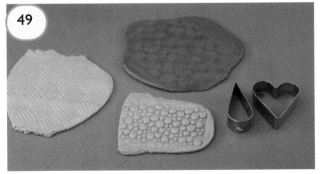

Roll a piece of each cane to 1.5cm diameter and cut two 5mm slices. Mould the two slices into leaf shapes, making the bottom of each ear quite pointed as this is going to be inserted into the owl head. You can have larger or smaller ears, make them droop or stand up, or even decorate them.

The Owl Wings:

I tend to now make my owl wings in a plain colour, texture them, then use gilder paste to highlight the texture. I find that the owls' feathers are very detailed so plainer wings stand out. However, I will also show you other designs.

49

Roll out the clay on PM1 and texture each one. You can either use bought texture sheets or rollers, or you could texture with anything you have around the house. It's amazing how many things can be used as texture-makers!

To make the wings I use a 2.5cm wide heart cutter, or a 3cm long teardrop cutter. If you use the heart, cut 2 for each owl. For the teardrop cut 6 for each owl.

The hearts are left as they are. For the teardrops, place one in the centre, then place the other two slightly overlapping either side and put a small ball of clay in a different colour at the top.

If you are using gilder paste, it might be a good idea to put it on the middle teardrop before adding the other two as it is difficult to get it in the small gap once cured. Leave the other two, they will be gilder pasted when cured.

If you don't have gilder paste, you can use other things to highlight your wings, eg eye shadow, mica powder, paint.

To cure them, cut a toilet roll in half lengthways and put the wings on it. This gives them a natural curve and they sit on the owls far better.

Some other ideas for wings.

Curing the stomachs, eyes, ears and wings:

Pre-heat the oven to $130°$ C. Put the stomach, eyes, ears and wings in for 25 minutes. Take out after this time and leave to cool.

Once cool, work out which stomach, eyes, ears and wings are going to be for each owl.

Making the feet:

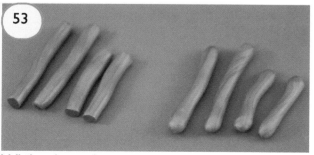

While the other parts are curing, make the feet. Roll gold clay to a log of 5mm diameter.

For each owl cut 2 x 5cm pieces and 2 x 4cm pieces (left picture).
Round both ends of each piece (right picture).
See page 21 for how to do this.

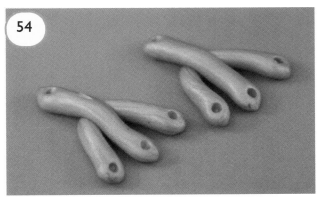

Bend the 5cm pieces into a U shape, and place the 4cm over the top. Using a large knitting needle, make a hole at the end of each toe.

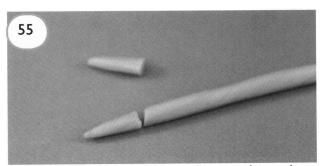

Roll out a 4mm diameter log in the colour you'd like to make the claws in. With your first finger, gently roll the end to a point and cut off 8mm. Make 8 of these pieces for each owl.

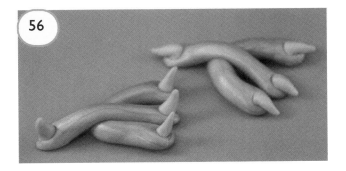

Gently push the blunt ends of the claws into the holes in the toes. Once in, carefully press down. You don't want to leave the claws sticking out too much as they will be in danger of being broken off.

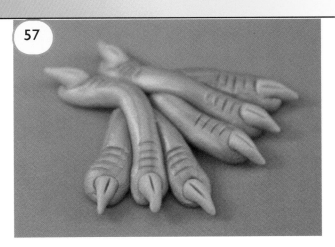

To finish off the feet, push the middles of the feet together, fanning out the toes. With the blunt side of any cutter make little marks along each toe and put a line in the claws. I find it helpful to put the feet on a smaller tile and make the owl up on the tile as it can be moved round more easily and you can get to all sides of the owl.

I love making owls with two or three different coloured toes, and you can change the colour of the feet, the one in front is using 18k gold clay.

Putting it all together:

Before you start, reduce all your canes until they measure 1.5cm diameter. Then cover them in ultra-fine glitter, as shown on page 21.

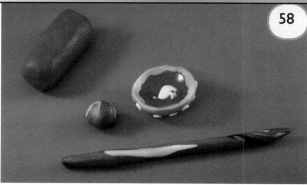

Take one of the owl bodies, a stomach, some scrap clay and the Bake & Bond. Roll some scrap clay into a ball around 1cm diameter, and some more scrap clay into a log. Put some Bake & Bond on the underside of the stomach.

Press the ball of clay into the back of the stomach and press into the base of the body. Make sure that the bottom of the stomach is in line with the bottom of the body. Also look at the stomach and decide which way it looks the best before pushing on firmly.

Take the log of scrap clay and fill in the gaps between the stomach and the owl body. This won't be seen but it provides a smooth surface of the feathers to adhere to.

Push the eyes into the head where you want them to sit, then remove them. This will leave an indentation of the eyes and will help you know where to put the feathers.

Take a cane, I've used the watercolour cane, roll it to 1.5cm in diameter and pinch one end to make a point. Cut 8 very thin slices.

These thin slices are going to be used to hide the scrap clay at the bottom of the owl. Place the first one just slightly overlapping the stomach with the fatter end uppermost and the pointed end going underneath the owl.

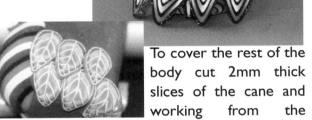

To cover the rest of the body cut 2mm thick slices of the cane and working from the bottom, place a row of slices, pointed end downwards, trying where possible to place a cane slice in between the two slices below. Continue up the owl, covering it completely apart from the eye sockets, until you reach the top. Do not cover the flat part of the head   .

This owl shows it more clearly. Note that the first leaf slice is just overlapping the stomach.

The bottom of the owl is now well covered.

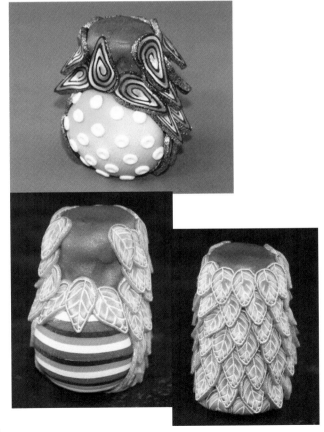

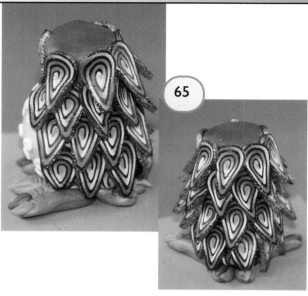

Push the ears in firmly.

It's now time to put your owl on his feet. Make sure that he is pressed firmly onto the feet, and that he is not leaning backwards or forwards. Check that he has his two toes showing behind him, and in the middle, and that his toes in the front are also centred.

Next are the ears. With a medium size knitting needle, make two holes in the top of the head, about 1 cm deep. Put some Bake & Bond in each hole as this will glue the ears in.

Continue adding rows of feathers, starting from the last row you did and working upwards. You can either cover the front up completely, like the owl on the top, or leave the eye sockets clear, as shown on the owl on the bottom. I like the size of feathers on the bottom owl best.

To make the beak, take a pea size ball of gold clay and with your thumbs and first fingers, gently roll each end so they make two soft points. Place this between the two eyes.

To put in the eyes, first blob some Bake & Bond onto the back of each owl eye, then carefully place them on the owl, holding your other hand flat against the back of the owl to push against, which will slightly flatten the feathers, but will keep you from ruining any by holding the owl with your fingertips.

If you have particularly fluffed out feathers and want to keep them like that, the best thing to do is put the eyes on once the wings are in place, then hold the wings firmly against the owl body as you push in the eyes.

If the beak is mostly on cured clay, put some Bake & Bond on it before fitting on the owl. To make nostrils, either poke two small holes in the top of the beak, or put two very small balls of clay on the beak and make holes in each.

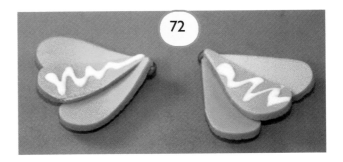

Put some Bake & Bond on the underside of each wing on the middle part if you've used teardrops, or all over if you've used hearts.

Using gilder paste on the wings:

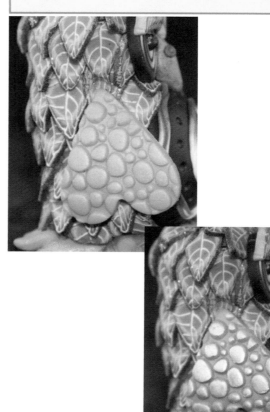

Push both wings on at the same time making sure they are level and look nice from all angles. Your owl is now ready to cure, unless you want to make a bowler hat, in which case make the hat first before curing.

Making a bowler hat:

To make a bowler hat as I've done here, roll out black clay on PM1 and cut out 2 x 2cm circles. On one circle slightly flatten all round the edge, this is the bottom of the hat.

For the top part, roll the second circle into a ball, then a little log, flattening the two ends. Place the bottom part on the head first, followed by the top part. I like to decorate it with slices of the leaf cane and three small red balls that look like berries.

Once the owl is cured and cooled take some gilder paste and put a little on some cloth - I use my finger, it washes off - and carefully rub it over the wing. The paste highlights the parts of the pattern that stand proud. I finish all my owls by varnishing them.

Make all your owls in the same way, but obviously in whatever arrangement of feathers, stomachs, eyes, ears and wings you like. Have fun with them, each one has its own little character, and you may even find yourself talking to them like I do!

79

Owls made by friends:

My sister Ruth's owl, showing its beautiful colourful feathers. She says I'm the 'arty' one, but this owl shows she's pretty creative herself. It's one of my favorite owls.

Three owls by my talented friend Tracy Marriott who always puts her own twist on my designs and comes up with something quite unique. I love claying with Tracy, she always inspires me to try different things.

Another friend, Ruth Peck, made these two owls. She always goes home and makes lots more of whatever we've made in the group - it's very satisfying watching someone progress so quickly.

These three owls were made by my friend Linda Hyam who really went to town with leaf canes. Linda is the cane queen of our group, she loves making them, has a great sense of colour, and practices at home. I love the detail in theses owls.

Our newest clay group member, Belinda Elliott made this lovely owl. She lives near Linda, so they get sneaky practice sessions in!

Turtles:

Turtles are quick and fun to make, I once made nearly **50** as wedding favours for my friend Mikey. They are a great way to use spare bits of cane, and can be decorated in many different ways. Enjoy!

TOOLS & MATERIALS:
for four turtles above

- Pasta machine
- Oven to cure clay in
- Acrylic or metal clay roller
- Needle tool / cocktail stick
- Sculpey Bake & Bond, or other liquid clay adhesive
- Good quality tin foil
- A silicone rubber shaping tool (optional but useful)
- A small ball tool approx 1mm diameter (I buy a pack of four for £1 in Poundland-type shops, in the nail manicure section)
- Circle cutters 4cm, 3cm and 8mm diameter
- Circle cutter 5mm (3/16") diameter (optional)
- 8 x 4mm black glass beads (2 per turtle)
- Knitting needle – I use a 7mm diameter one
- A small tile 9.5cm square to cure each turtle on (this is optional but very useful. I buy them at Homebase for 16p each)
- 600 grit wet and dry sandpaper – from any DIY store
- Polymer clay varnish. I use Darwi Vernis – optional

- Tissue blade
- Tile to work on
- Tin foil

CLAY:
for four turtles above

- 1 x 56g white clay

- 1 x 56g of any other coloured clay. I used Premo Sculpey Accents Peacock Pearl

- 1/2 x 56g black clay

- Approximately 100g of scrap clay (equivalent to two 56g blocks) – this is for four turtles, if you're only making one you need around 25g of scrap clay

Making the Shell:

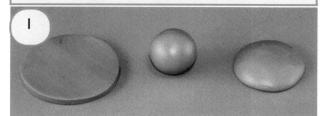

Roll some scrap clay on PM0 and cut a 4cm circle. Roll this into a ball then push round the edges, making it into a dome shape, 3cm diameter. Make four and put to one side until you've make the canes.

Making the Skinner blend for the canes:

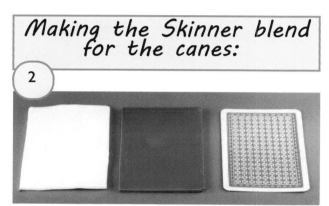

Roll some white clay, and another colour clay on PM0 and cut to the shape of a standard playing card, 9cm x 6cm.

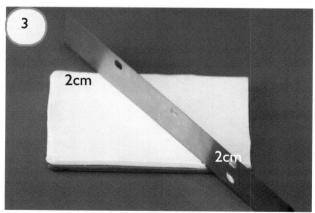

2cm

2cm

Put the white clay on top of the other clay and measure 2cm from the top left corner, and 2cm from the bottom right as shown. Cut through then separate the four pieces of clay and put the two white pieces together, and the two coloured pieces together.

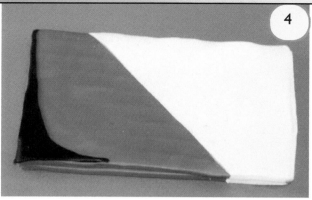

Take some black clay and roll out on PM6 then cut a shape as above, 3cm along the bottom edge and going to a point at the top. This is a technique adapted from Ivy Niles, an incredible clayer who makes beautiful canes. Doing this gives a darker end to the blend.

Now follow steps 3 to 5 on page 18 to make your Skinner blend.

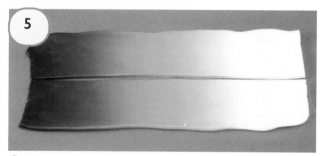

Once you are happy with your blend, cut the clay in half as shown.

Making the Skinner blend Jelly Roll cane:

Roll some black clay on PM5, lay one half of the blend on it and cut round.
Roll out some white clay on PM5 and lay the black/blended clay sheet on it and cut round.

7

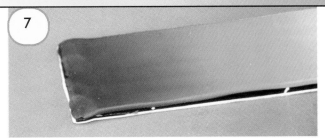

Before putting through the pasta machine, pinch one of the short ends; this stops the three layers of clay separating when you put it through the pasta machine.

8

Put the clay though the pasta machine, pinched edge first on PMO.

9

Roll the clay, lighter end first, with the thin white layer on the outside.

Reduce the cane to 1.5cm diameter and cut in half. Your Skinner blend jelly roll cane is now completed.

Making the Skinner blend Bull's Eye cane:

10

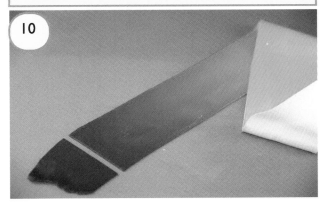

Take the second half of the Skinner blend and put it lengthways through the pasta machine on PM1 then PM3 and if your clay isn't too sticky, PM5. Before rolling, cut a small piece off the darker end, around 2cm.

11

Roll the cut off piece of clay into a log the width of the strip of clay and place at the dark end before rolling up.

12

You're now going to cover your bull's eye cane with a layer of black, then white, then coloured clay, all on PM5. Follow steps 1 to 2 on page 22 for how to do this.

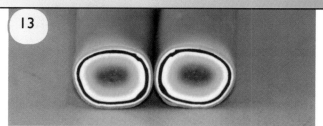

Roll the cane to 1.5cm diameter and cut in half. Your Skinner blend bull's eye cane is now completed.

Making the shells:

There are two ways you can make the shells, the first is to roll out some clay on PM3 and cut a 4cm circle. Cover the dome with this as shown.

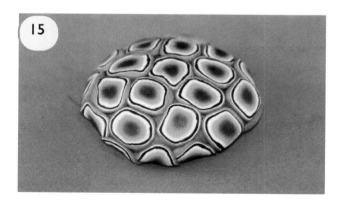

Take one of the bull's eye canes and roll to 8mm diameter, then cut thin slices off and place all over the dome, making sure you go round the edge to underneath. This is because the edge of the shell will be seen.

You now need to decide if you like the pattern as it is, or would like it smoother.

If you want your turtle shell smoother, which I like, first push the edges of the canes together, hiding the underneath clay, then take the knitting needle and roll it over the whole shell until it is smooth. When you've finished, make sure that the shell is still only 3cm diameter. If it is larger, it can look out of proportion.

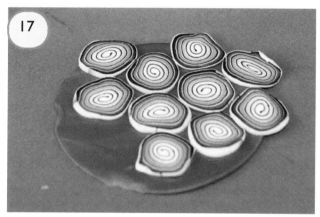

The second way to make the shells is to roll out some clay, on PM3 and cut a 4cm circle. Cover the circle with thin slices of the jelly roll cane.

Once covered, smooth all the joins as before, pushing together with your fingers and then rolling gently, but this time with your clay roller. Finally re-cut the 4cm circle.

19

black clay rolled on PM3. Cut 8mm slices of the bull's eye cane and place at intervals over the shell. Finally, with your ball tool, make little texture marks all over the shell between the cane slices. The ball tool texture is better done just before curing, but I finished it now so you could see what the shell looks like.

Place the dome in the middle of the covered circle and fold over all the way round.

20

The final shell is made from a mixture of bull's eye and jelly roll cane slices, and a 3mm diameter roll of lighter clay is put round the base of the shell.

Your second shell is now covered.

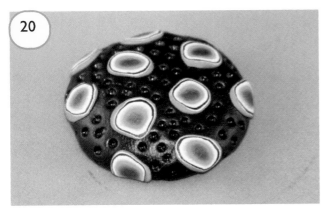

20

21

For the third shell cover with a 4cm circle of

Now we're going to shape the shell to allow for the head, legs and tail to sit nicely under it. Take your large knitting needle and make an indentation where the head is going to be.

Check that the clay on the top hasn't cracked, if it has, smooth it out before continuing.

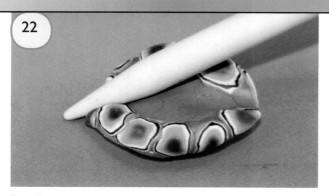

Finally make two further indentations each side, between the head and tail for the two front legs and two back legs. You should now have six indentations, fairly evenly spaced, with the largest one for the head, and smallest for the tail. This is the best time to put any indentations in the shell.

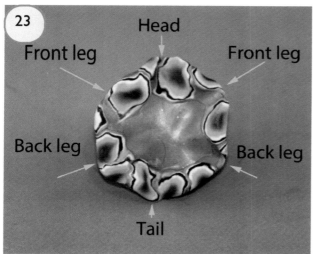

23

Head

Front leg

Front leg

Back leg

Back leg

Tail

At the opposite end make a smiliar indentation, but with the smaller part of the needle. This is going to be for the tail and doesn't have to be as large as the head.

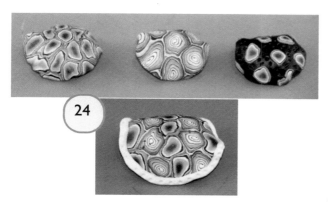

24

The shells are ready to be cured. Follow manufacturers' recommended temperatures and times for whichever clay you have, but as a guide, for Fimo or Premo I preheat the oven to 130°C and cure them for 30 minutes.

I like to put them in a bed of cornflour as this supports their shape and doesn't give any of the shiny patches that you get if clay is in contact with a tile, but they can also be cured on some paper.

After they're cured and cooled, sand the shells with some 600 grit wet and dry sandpaper, keeping the paper and shells wet with warm water. Make sure you rinse well afterwards to remove any clay. Sanding is optional, but it really helps give the shell a smooth finish, and if you're either buffing or varnishing, sanding is a must. If you're buffing later, I would suggest also sanding with 800 and 1000 grit.

Making the head, legs and tail:

25

Roll some scrap clay into a log, 1cm diameter and 12cm long.

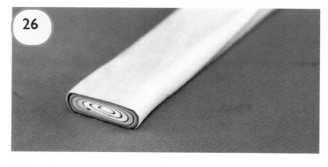

26

Take the remaining piece of jelly roll cane and roll to 1cm diameter. Cut in half and flatten one half as shown above.

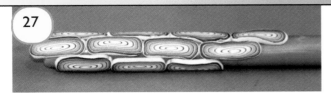

27

Cut some thin slices of the elongated jelly roll and place on the log in a brick-like pattern. Cover the whole log.

28

Once covered, spend some time gently pushing the slices together, hiding the scrap clay underneath, then roll to smooth. Lastly roll so that the diameter of the cane is 1cm again.

29

Cut the following sizes:
1 x 3.5cm - for the head
2 x 2.5cm - for the front legs
2 x 2cm - for the back legs
1 x 1cm - for the tail

30

Now you're going to round one end of each of the pieces. To do this, using your thumb and first (index) finger gently pinch the edges of the cane upwards and inwards. Then repeat on the other two edges, drawing the edges in to cover the scrap clay. It will take four to six pinches to complete, then smooth the end.

31

The completed pieces, with one end rounded each.

32

For two of the turtles cover the log with a thin layer of coloured clay, and the fourth one cover with a thin layer of black clay, then cut to size and round the ends as before.

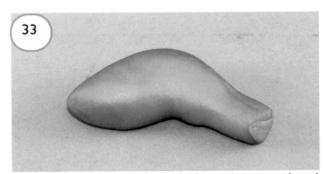

33

Take the largest piece and shape it into a head as shown. Make the non-rounded end fairly narrow as this is going underneath the shell.

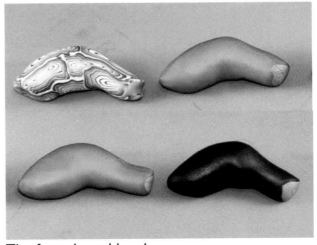

The four shaped heads.

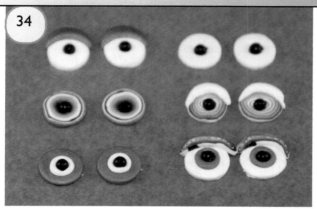

To make the eyes you have the choice to use slices of the canes, or cut circles of clay. Use a 8mm diameter circle cutter to cut circles of clay that have been rolled out on PM3. If you want to make eyebrows, use the 8mm cutter as below:

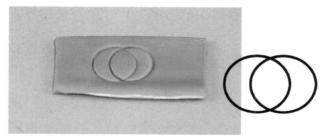

Overlapping the circles in this way ensures two identical pieces, which you then put on top of the eyes. In the bottom two pairs of eyes, there is a 5mm circle as well as the 8mm. Finish the eyes by inserting a 4mm black glass bead in each eye. Put on the turtle's head.

For the nostrils, roll two small balls of clay and place at the end of the head. Make a hole with either a needle tool, a cocktail stick, or the ball tool.

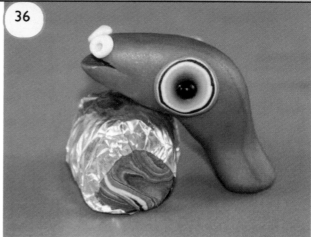

For the mouth, make a cut, then slightly pinch the bottom lip to make it protrude a little.

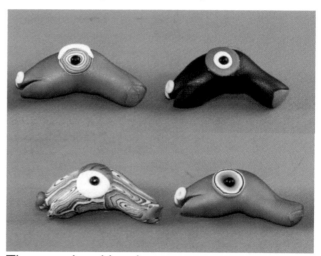

The completed heads.

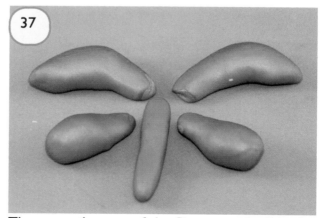

These are the rest of the flippers and tail in the arrangement you're going to put them on the turtle shell. Notice the tail is quite long, this is so it joins all the other pieces together.

38

Before you put the turtle together, prepare the underbelly. To make this roll out some clay on PM1 and cut a 3cm circle. Pull it gently into an egg shape.

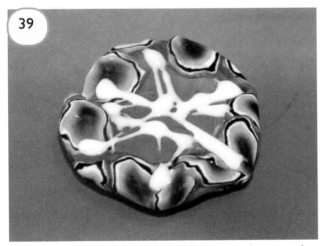

39

Put Bake & Bond, or whichever polymer clay adhesive you use, on the underside of the shell.

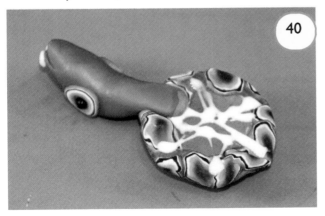

40

Start by putting the head on the shell, followed by the front legs, back legs and the tail. Notice in the next picture how I've made the tail longer and thinner, this helps adhere all the pieces.

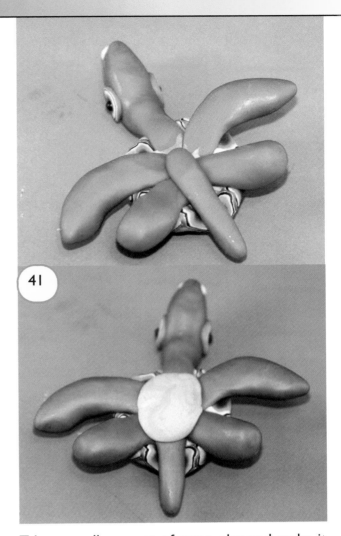

41

Take a small amount of scrap clay and make it into a flat disc, placing it in the middle of the underside of the turtle. This creates a smoother surface for the underbelly to go on.

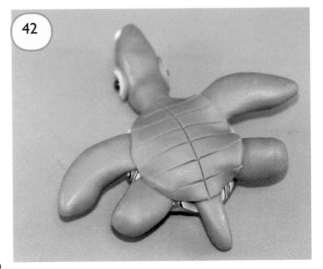

42

Place the underbelly on, making sure that it touches the shell in all the gaps between the head / legs / tail. To make the lines, use the blunt side of your tissue blade.

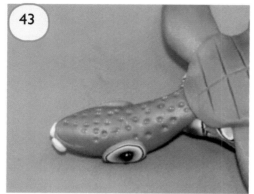

If you plan to texture your turtle, it's best to do this to the underside of its head at this point as it's more difficult once it's on the tile.

Now put your turtle on a small tile. Roll some tin foil into a log and place under the head to support it until it's cured. Finish texturing the rest of the head, the legs and tail with your ball tool, and lift the tail. You can leave the turtle like this or decorate it further.

For the second turtle I used the jelly roll head etc. and put them with the plainer of the shells. I've also given the turtle more movement by lifting the right front leg and the left back, using foil to support, so he looks like he's swimming.

For the third turtle, I've decorated his head and legs with small slices of the two canes, put his head slightly to the right, and curled his tail.

For the final turtle I've again decorated with slices of cane, and also 5mm circles.

Finally cure the turtles in the same way you cured the shells. Leave to cool completely and they're finished. You can varnish with a polymer clay varnish, if you like your turtles shiny. I use Darwi vernis.

GALLERY

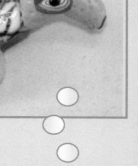

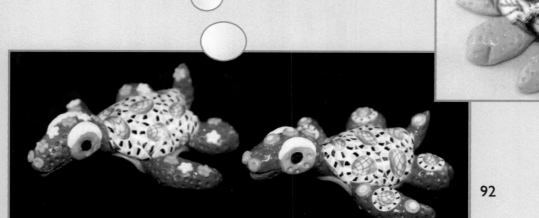

TOOLS & MATERIALS:

- Pasta machine
- Tissue blade
- Acrylic or metal clay roller
- Needle tool / cocktail stick
- Tile to work on
- Oven to cure clay in
- Cutters – I use a variety of circle cutters, and some star ones too
- Sculpey Ultra-light clay to make moulds
- Gilder paste in gold, bronze and silver
- Black acrylic paint
- Paintbrush
- Tools for texture, eg:
  - dentist tool
  - toothbrush
  - threaded bar
  - ball tools
- Materials for texture, eg:
  - buttons
  - plastic packing material
  - washing up scourer
  - commercial texture makers
- Optional – metal watch parts, chain, eyelets
- Optional – glue on diamontes
- Optional – Polymer clay varnish. I use Darwi Vernis satin

Steampunk is a Victorian era style with steam-powered futuristic technology. It began as a sub-genre of science fiction and fantasy literature, originally by H.G. Wells and Jules Verne, but has developed in recent years to become a craft and lifestyle movement that commonly features some aspect of steam-powered machinery.

Ladies wear corsets, gentlemen wear suit vests, it's all very classy!

Steampunk art is as varied and eccentric as your imagination; common items found in art and craft designs include clockwork gadgets and jewelry, top hats, corsets, weapons, metal nuts, bolts and screws, goggles, hearts, zips, belts, butterflies and other insects, wings, rivets, and lots of texture that looks like metal.

CLAY:

The colours I use for steampunk are all the metallic ones such as:

- Premo Sculpey Accents Gold
- Premo Sculpey Accents 18k Gold
- Premo Sculpey Accents Bronze
- Premo Sculpey Copper
- Premo Sculpey Accents Silver
- Premo Sculpey Accents Antique Gold
- Any other type of metalic clay eg Fimo
  I also add accent colours of non -metalic clay

Making your own texture moulds:

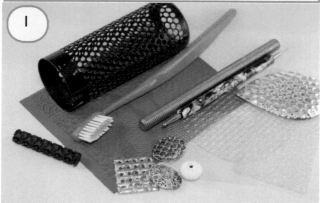

First gather the tools and materials that you are going to use for texture. This can be anything: the large round cylinder is from a cheap roller hair brush, the short black roller is a Kor tool, the plastic sheets were found in various packages eg the bottom of plastic meat containers. At the bottom of the picture we have various beads, broaches and buttons, I have great fun scouring the charity shops for these.

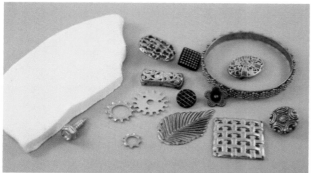

Look for anything with an interesting shape or pattern to make moulds out of, again charity shops are a wonderful source for jewellery.

To make the moulds I use Sculpey Ultralight clay.
To condition it mix with your hands rather than the pasta machine. It's very soft and easy to condition.

Roll your clay out to approximately 7mm thick and place the metal items face down in it, pushing them well in so they make a good indentation.

Cut round each piece, leaving a gap all the way round. Don't spend ages making nice even cuts, the only important part is the mould in the middle.

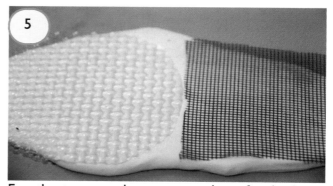

For the texture sheets, press them firmly down into the clay, before lifting off prior to curing.

To make straps, use something like an old

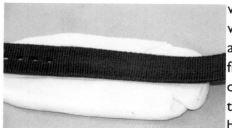

webbing watch strap and press it firmly into the clay. Remove the strap before curing.

94

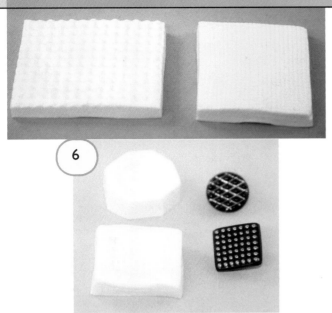

6

Other textures and embellishments:

You can either leave the metal parts in the clay to cure, or take them out. Remove any items that aren't metal, such as the plastic texture sheet, and then cure the moulds at 130°C for 30 minutes. If you've left the metal pieces in to cure, remove them when the clay is cold.

You can also texture sheets of clay by pressing various items into them, this amazing raised dot pattern was made by using a replacement hair brush inner, bought very cheaply from a chemist.

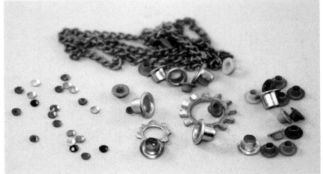

As well as making moulds and textures for clay, you can add other things such as hot glue diamantes, metal chain, eyelets and washers.

These are watch parts, very popular in steampunk designs, but quite expensive. I tend to use them sparingly, preferring to make my own decorations when possible.

Silicone moulds are also great to use. This is a favourite of mine from Marie Segal.

You can see above how effective the moulds are once metalic clay is used in them. Each photo shows the metal item, the mould, and the clay once it's been pressed into the mould.

95

Making the steampunk parts:

As well as textures, moulds and additions, I like to make a variety of metal looking items: screws, nuts, gears, texture plates etc with just metalic clay. Every time I make a new one I put it on a piece of clay so I build up a 'library' of ideas. I roll the clay out to around PM2 or PM3 before cutting to shape, apart from the items that have more than one component, when I roll the clay on PM5 for the top parts.

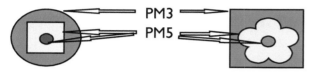

This is my tool kit for making steampunk.
1. Clay roller
2. Clay blade
3. Various sized ball tools
4. Pointed tools
5. Circle cutters in a variety of different sizes
6. Other cutters including stars and hearts
7. A dentist tool
8. A craft knift
9. Small screwdrivers with different shaped ends

Many of the items on the previous photograph were made from using cutters in various sizes, then embellishing using ball tools, the dentist tool, a needle tool or a screwdriver.

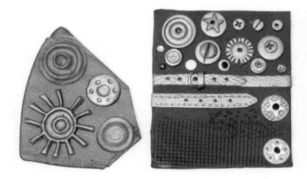

The shapes on the left were made from moulds that I made.

The one on the left shows various types of texture, while the one on the right shows predominently the flower and star cutter designs.

Making straps:

I love making straps. First cut a strip of either textured (bottom) or non-textured brown clay to the size you want. On the non-textured clay make little holes along the edges to look like stitching.

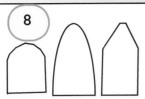

8 Now cut another strip, textured or stitched to match the first strap, and the same width. Make one end rounded or pointed.

9

With a needle tool, make some holes along the middle of the strap, evenly spaced.

10

Cut another strip of clay, around a third of the width of the strap; this is going to be the keeper that fits after the buckle. Texture it the same as the other two straps.

Lay the pointed strap on top of the first strap, and cut a piece of wire, around twice the width of the strap. Bend the wire at each end so it fits round the strap. Place it just above one of the holes.

Then cut another short piece of wire and push it into the hole. Cut it so it just overlaps the bent wire.

Finally place the thin piece of clay - the keeper - over the strap and cut it so that it goes over the edges.

The Process:

11

I'm going to show you how I made the steampunk sign at the beginning of this tutorial as it will show you the steps taken to achieve the 'industrial and oily' look. I started by making the word 'Steampunk' in light gold clay, texturing each letter differently and making the 'a' into a strap.

12

Now make lots of bits to go round the words. These are the ones I used in the design, along with lots of different textures.

13

This is the finished piece. I've used Premo accents silver, bronze and copper, with just the occassional bit of gold as I want the words to stand out.

14

Next you need some black acrylic paint, a paint brush, some kitchen paper and wet wipes.

15

Paint the black acrylic paint all over the steampunk, making sure it gets into all the crevices and holes.

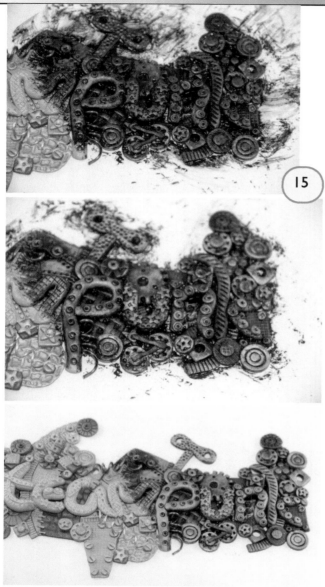

Finally, using the gilder paste, highlight the various parts. I use silver, gold and bronze to do this.

This is the finished piece. Notice I've added spirals of wire (wire wrapped round needles and cocktail sticks).

Making a steampunk chicken:

Using the kitchen towel, wipe away the black paint. Take as much off as you can with the kitchen paper before finishing with the wet wipes. Be careful with these as it's easy to wipe off too much paint and lose the blackened look.

16

Make the beak and feet with a steampunk theme, I've made some examples here. The beak on the left was inspired by Christi Friesen's steampunk book. The rest of the chicken is made the same way as the tutorial on page 23 but covered in steampunk rather than canes.

Hearts and pendants following a workshop with the lovely Marie

Steampunk Christmas tree decoration.

The turtle was made using techniques from Christi Friesen's Steampunk book

Terence the turtle, again inspired by Christi Friesen. I've added clock parts to these, and given him goggles - so he can go flying!!

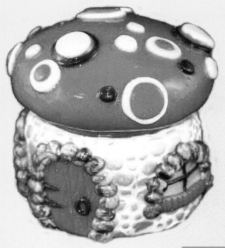

TOOLS & MATERIALS:

- Pasta machine
- Tissue blade
- Acrylic or metal clay roller
- Needle tool / cocktail stick
- A craft knife
- Tile to work on
- Oven to cure clay in
- A small glass jar – I save the little jam ones from cream teas!
- A standard playing card, or a piece of card measuring 9cm x 6cm
- A small ball tool approx 1 – 2mm diameter I buy a pack of four from £1 shops, they're in the nail manicure section
- 4cm circle cutter
- Optional circle cutters that I also use, but are not necessary in order to make the fairy houses: 6cm and 7cm Fat Daddio cutters, 3cm, 15mm, 12mm, 9mm, 7mm, and 5mm diameter metal or plastic cutters
- Knitting needles – I use 7mm diameter and 4mm diameter ones
- Sculpey Bake & Bond
- Polymer clay varnish. I use Darwi Vernis

CLAY:

For each house you will need around 30g of scrap clay for the roof.

For the blue/yellow fairy house:
- 1/2 x 56g cream coloured clay
- 1/2 x 56g block of one colour (I've used blue)
- 1/2 a 56g block of another colour (I've used yellow)
- A small amount of white (about the size of a walnut)

For the red fairy house:
- 1/2 a 56g block of red clay – I like Premo Sculpey Pomegranate
- 1/2 a 56g block of white clay
- A small amount of black clay (about the size of a walnut)

OPTIONAL:

- A Kor pebble texture roller for the red fairy house. Other makes are available
- Ultra fine glitter for canes
- Various 5mm (3/16") cutters – flower, heart, petal, star
- Gilder paste. I use silver, but you could use paint, eye shadow, ultra fine glitter or mica powder instead

Making the lid:

Take some conditioned scrap clay and roll it out on PM0. Cut 2 x 4cm diameter circles and roll both together into a ball, then roll out to a circle 6cm diameter. If you have a 6cm circle cutter you can use this to make the circle.

Place the lid in the middle of the circle of clay.

Place the lid in the middle of the circle, and gently mould the clay round and under the lid edge. Don't worry about clay covering the part that screws onto the jar, this will be trimmed later.

Make sure that there are no air bubbles in the top of the lid. Use your blade to make a slit in any bubbles and remove the air before smoothing.

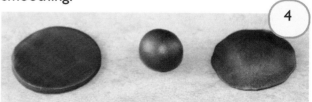

Roll scrap clay out on PM0 and cut a 4cm circle. Roll this into a ball, then mould into a dome shape, approximately 3cm diameter.

Take the domed clay and place it in the middle of the lid. Next smooth round the edge of the dome so it blends into the clay on the lid. This will make a nicer finish to the coloured layer.

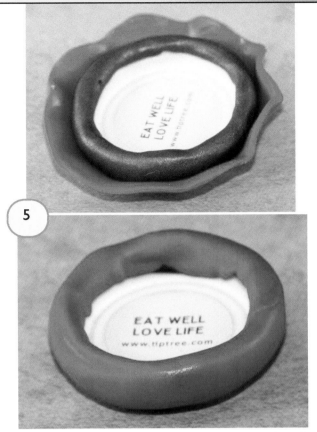

Take clay in the colour you want to make the lid and roll out on PM3. Cut a 7cm diameter circle and cover the lid, making sure that the clay goes all the way round the lid and underneath as shown.

Using a craft knife, carefully pare away the spare clay from the lid. Put on the jar once more and again cut away any spare clay. Your lid is now ready for adding the spots.

Screw the covered lid onto the jar tightly. When you take it off you will be able to see the clay that needs to be removed.

Making a graduated coloured lid:

I thought I'd show you how to make a graduated coloured lid first as it uses less clay than the blue and yellow house shown later on in this tutorial and I use this a lot to make my fairy houses.

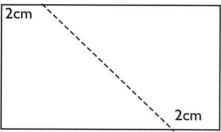

Take a standard sized playing card, or piece of card 9cm x 6cm, and cut it in half, as shown above.

Roll the colour clay of choice, and white clay on PM0 Use the left half of the card as a template for the coloured clay, and the right half of the card as a template for the white clay. Put together the two halves as shown above. Now follow steps 1 to 4 on page 18 to make an increased dark Skinner blend.

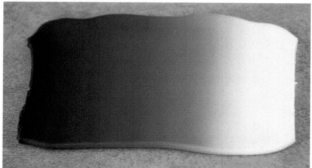

The finished blend. Now put this through the pasta machine on PM1, then PM3, making sure you put it through with the strips vertical. You want the clay thinner but the stripes the same width so they all fit on the lid.

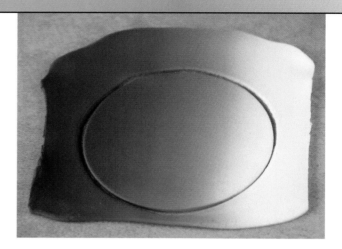

Either using a 7cm diameter circle cutter, or making a card template and cutting round it, cut a circle of clay, trying to ensure that you get a good blend of both dark and light colour. Cover as you did for the red lid, steps 5 - 7.

You're now ready to add the spots.

For the graduated lid, take the remaining piece of graduated clay and cut circles in a variety of sizes. For the red lid make a variety of sizes circles in red, white and black.

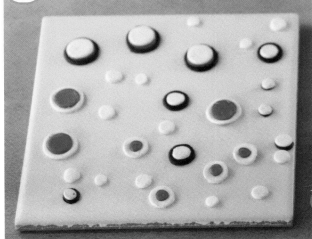

I find it easier to put the lids on the jars when putting the spots on. Once finished, cure in the oven, 130 °C for 30 minutes. You can either cure them on the jars, or place them in a container filled with cornflour which will support them without distorting or marking the lids.

I made a ladybird because one of the lids cracked when cured, and the ladybird covered up the crack nicely! Take some red clay and some black clay and roll out on PM5. Cut a 15mm circle in both colours, then using the same 15mm cutter, cut a small piece out of each circle as shown. Put the small black piece on the red body as shown above.

Roll some scrap clay out on PM5 and cut a 15mm circle. Roll into a ball then flatten it a little, and cover it with the red & black circle.

With the back of your tissue blade, make a mark down the middle of the red part. Next place small black dots either side of the line, and finally put two little holes in the black head for eyes. If you have already cured your lid, make sure you use clay adhesive to attach the ladybird before curing again.

105

The finished lid, complete with strategically placed ladybirds!

Fairy house.
Using a texture tool:

I use a Kor texture tool for this, but if you don't have one you could use anything to make texture, such as a toothbrush, peach stones, the side of bottle tops, lace doilies, buttons, the list is endless.

First roll out some clay on PM3 and cut to the height of the jar you are covering. You don't want it to go right to the top as it will stop the lid screwing on.

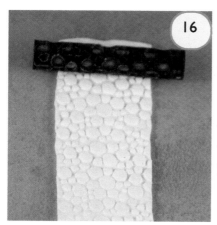

Roll the texture roller along the clay, or use whatever texture maker you are using.

Carefully place the strip round your glass jar, cutting to size and butting the two edges together.

At this point you can highlight the texture by using gilder paste, spread a very small amount lightly on top of the clay and it will really make the texture 'pop'. You could use other mediums such as ultra fine glitter, oil paint, or eyeshadow.

Using a craft knife, cut the shape of a door out of the clay wall. Use this cut out piece as a template for the door.

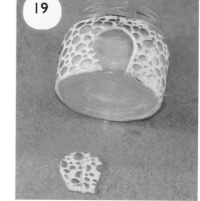

20

Insert the door into the clay wall. I've made a wood grain effect on the door.

21

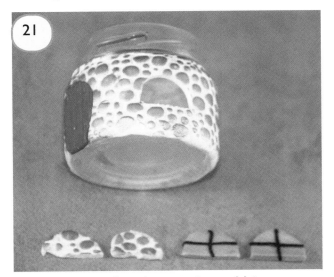

Do the same for the windows. Using a very thin roll of black, or other darker colour, make a cross on each window to show window panes before replacing in the clay wall.

22

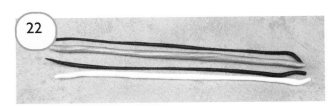

To make the stones that surround the door and windows, start by rolling some white, black and silver/grey clay into thin logs.

23 | **a**

(a) Roll the logs together and twist.

b

(b) Fold in half and twist again.

c

(c) Roll to lengthen....

d

(d).... and twist again.

e

(e) Fold in three, twist, and push together.

24

Flatten slightly with the clay roller before putting through the pasta machine on PM3. cut 5mm (3/16") circles.

25

Roll each circle into a ball, make around 45.

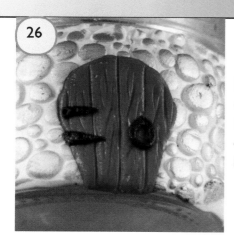

26

Decorate the door with hinges and a door knocker.

The completed house.

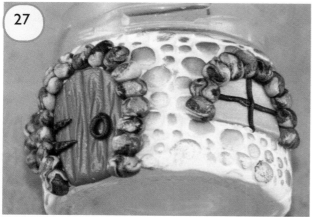

27

Place the balls round the door and the top arch of each window.

28

Roll out some red clay and cut a strip to fit at the bottom of the window as a window sill. Cure 30 mins at 130° C.

Fairy house· Stone cottage:

29

Start by making the door and windows for the fairy house.

Place the door and windows onto the jar.

30

108

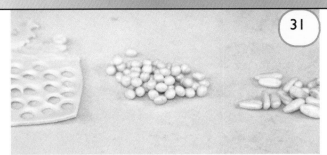

Roll out some cream coloured clay on PM4 and cut out 5mm (3/16") circles. Roll them into balls. For the slightly larger stones that go round the door and window, roll together 2 circles, then roll them into a little log, as shown on the right.

First, lay the larger cream logs round the door and the tops of the windows as shown.

Now fill in the spaces using the smaller round balls, making sure that there are no gaps.

Stone cottage roof:

Start by covering the lid, following steps 1 - 4.

Then make a Skinner blend. Roll some blue and yellow clay on PM2 and cut each colour to the size of a playing card (9cm x 6cm). Follow steps 1 to 5 on pages 17 and 18 to make a Skinner blend.

Once you have the blend, cut it in half lengthways, and lay one peice on top of the other. Roll lengthways with your clay roller to make it slightly thinner.

Pinch one of the short ends and put through the pasta machine on PM0 with the pinched end first.

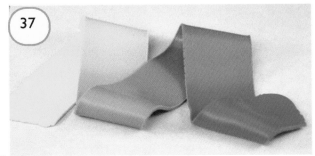

109

Put through on PM2, then PM4 and PM6 until you have a long thin ribbon.

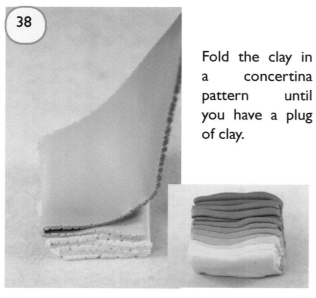

Fold the clay in a concertina pattern until you have a plug of clay.

Cut a peice off the plug, about a quarter of it. This is going to cover the lid. Roll it out using the clay roller first, then if liked, the pasta machine, until you can cut a 7cm diameter circle. Cover the lid as before.

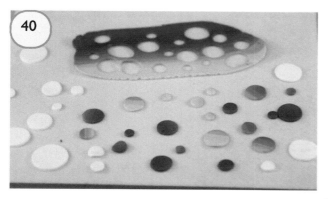

Using the off-cut from the lid, and if necessary cutting another slice from the plug and rolling thinly, cut a variety of sized circles. Also cut some in white. Make up spots as before and put on the lid.

The finished roof.

Leaf cane for the stone house:

Gently push the corners of the remaining plug into a circular shape.

42

Make four cuts through the plug.

43

Roll out some white clay on PM1 and cut a rectangle 7cm x 2.5cm. Roll out some black clay on PM6, lay the white clay on it and cut round. Lastly roll out some gold or light brown clay on PM1, lay the black clay on it and cut to shape. You now have a three layered rectangle.

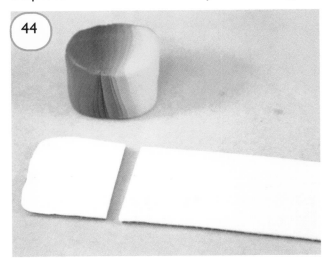

44

Pinch one of the short ends, then put through the pasta machine on PM0, then PM2. Fold in half, with the light brown on the inside, and put

through on PM0 again, then PM2. Cut a piece off, the same width as the plug, and put the remaining peice through the pasta machine on PM4.

45

Take one of the slices of the plug and place on the long strip. Cut round it, and replace on the plug.

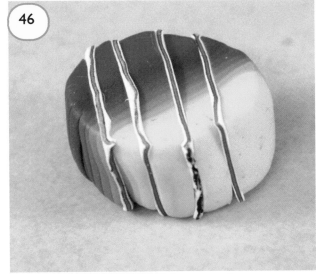

46

Repeat with all four sections.

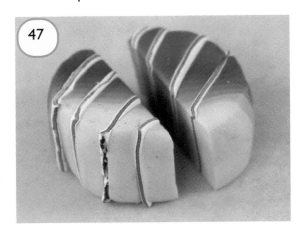

47

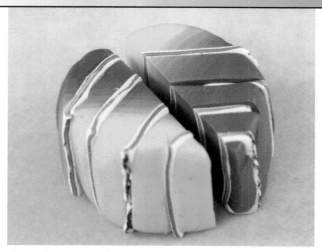

Cut the cane diagonally, then turn one of the halves round; this makes the leaf veins.

48

Taking the strip of clay you cut off earlier, pinch one end and place, with the pinched end at the top of the leaf, between the two halves.

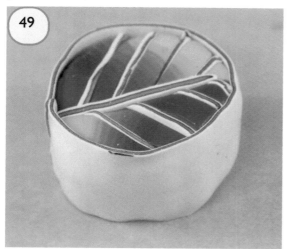

49

Take the remaining strip of clay and put it round the edge of the cane. Make it longer if needed, and cut it to a little wider than the cane. This allows for shrinkage once you lengthen the cane.

50

Lengthen the cane until it measures 1cm in diameter. Cut the cane in half.

51

You can cover the canes in ultra fine glitter at this point or leave them plain. To make the cane into a leaf shape pinch the top of the cane to make it into a leaf shape, then cut slices off it.

52

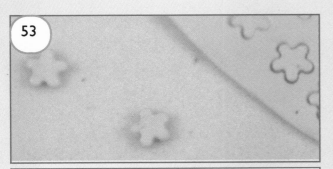

53

Arrange the leaves on the fairy house, adding little yellow flowers if desired, or if you don't have a flower cutter, little yellow balls look nice.

This house's roof was made using slices from a flower cane, with smaller slices making delphiniums.

The finished fairy house.

GALLERY

Pebbles highlighted with silver

Another stone fairy house, this time with a thatched roof and decorated with orange cane flowers.

I tend to make fairy houses when I learn a new technique, I made this one after I bought a tutorial on making denim polymer clay from Silvie Peraud.

GALLERY

This house's roof was made by covering the lid with a variety of leaves, berries, swirls, hearts and stars in various greens, then curing. After curing it was covered with black acrylic paint, then wiped off, leaving the paint in the indentations. Finally gilder paste in gold and bronze was used to highlight different parts.

Various sheets of clay were decorated using paint and silk screens, cut into strips and made into separate sheets of stripes or patchwork. These were then used to make the house on the left.

TOOLS & MATERIALS:
for one Darcy Dachshund

- Pasta machine   • Tile to work on
- Tissue blade and rigid blade
- Acrylic or metal clay roller
- Needle tool / cocktail stick
- Playing card or card 9cm x 6cm
- Oven to cure clay in
- Good quality tin foil – 30cm wide
- 18.5cm of 1mm wire – I get it from the garden centre or DIY store
- Circle cutter 6mm or 5mm diameter
- Oval cutters 2cm, 1.5mm and 12mm
- 2 x 4mm black glass beads
- Knitting needles – I use 7mm diameter and 4mm diameter ones
- Sculpey Bake & Bond, or other adhesive
- Polymer clay varnish. I use Darwi Vernis
- Clay extruder with 1.5mm round hole disc

CLAY:
Enough for one Darcy Dachshund

- 1/2 x 56g Premo Sculpey Accents Copper
- 1/2 x 56g Premo Sculpey Accents Antique Gold
- 1/2 x 56g Premo Sculpey Accents Bronze
- 1/2 x 56g Premo Sculpey Black
- Approximately 30g scrap clay

For the coat:
- 1/2 x 56g each of two colours of your choice

Darcy the Dachshund:

Nearly everyone in our family has a dog, and my mother had a gorgeous little dachshund called Darcy. I say little, because although he was meant to be a miniature, we called him a midi as he was halfway between a miniature and a standard! He accompanied us to horse events. He and mum are joined here by dad's Jack Russell Lucy, my Norfolk Terrier Jasper, and Bella the Deerhound.

GALLERY

115

Making the dachshund body:

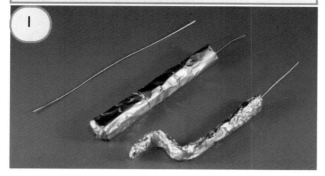

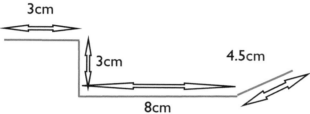

3cm

3cm

4.5cm

8cm

Take the 18.5cm piece of wire, then take the tin foil, and cut off a piece 42cm x 30cm. Fold it in three, making it 14cm wide, and wrap this round the wire, level with the left end, leaving 4.5cm bare wire on the right. Now you're going to fold it to the measurements shown in the diagram: 3cm, bend at a right angle, 3cm, bend at the opposite right angle, 8cm, bend slightly upwards - this is going to be the tail, bending it slightly helps keep the foil in place. Finally press the foil so it's compressed onto the wire.

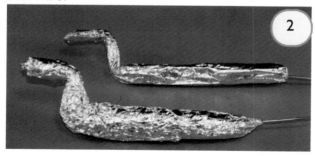

You now need to bulk out the body, neck and head. Take strips of foil, double thickness, and carefully build up the areas as shown above. Notice the top of the neck is still quite slim, but the chest is deeper, and the body tapers towards the tail. This is what you're aiming for.

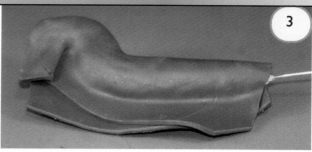

Condition and roll out some scrap clay on PM1. Drape it over the body, making sure you only cover the tin foil part, not the tail.

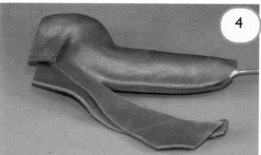

Trim the excess clay and smooth down all the joins.

This is the shape you're looking for. We are now going to further build up the head to give it that typical wire-haired 'Dachsy' square head.

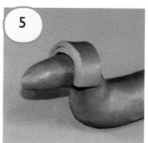

Roll clay on PM1 and lay 2 x 1.5cm wide strips over the back of the head as shown.

116

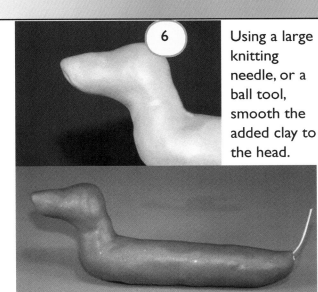

6 Using a large knitting needle, or a ball tool, smooth the added clay to the head.

You'll notice that the muzzle is slightly broader and at an angle. Add little bits of clay and smooth down until you have the above head shape.

Making the cane to cover the body:

7 Take the black, copper, bronze and antique gold clay and roll each one out on PM0. Cut each clay to the size of a standard playing card (9cm x 6cm).

Place the antique gold on the bronze, and the copper on the black, and cut diagonally, 2cm from each end as shown.

Separate the clay and match the colours - ie each colour has two thicknesses of clay - and put back as shown: the gold with the bronze, and the black with the copper. Now follow the Skinner Blend technique on pages 17 and 18, steps 1 to 5 to make the two blends.

The two completed blends.

8 Make sure that your two pieces are the same size, trim off the top and bottom and cut the rectangles into four equal pieces as shown.

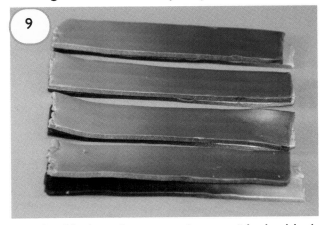

9 Put the black and copper pieces, with the black to the left, on the work surface and cover each piece with the gold and bronze clay, with the gold to the left.

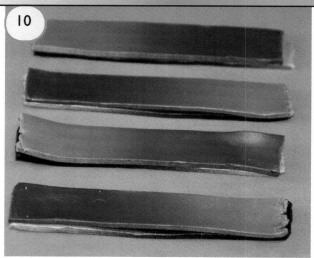

10

Put each strip lengthways, (shorter end first) through the pasta machine on PM0, then again on PM1. Turn the second and forth strips round so they look like the picture above.

> TIP: Before putting the strips through the pasta machine, pinch the end that is going through first. This will prevent the two parts separating.

11

Stack the strips in the following order:

Antique Gold - Bronze Black - Copper	
Bronze - Antique Gold Copper - Black	
Antique Gold - Bronze Black - Copper	
Bronze - Antique Gold Copper - Black	

12

Cut the stack in half.

Place one stack on top of the other.

13

Push the stack down until it measures about half the original height and is wider. It is now ready to use.

14

Trim the stack, keeping the off-cuts to use later, and cut the stack into slices approximately 3-4mm thick.

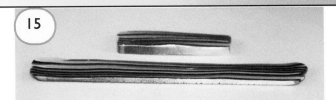

15

Next put each slice through the pasta machine on PM0 lengthways. Then again on PM1, and finally on PM2.

16

Put three slices side by side, and roll gently with your roller to join. Cover the dog with the slices, smoothing out any joins with a knitting needle or ball tool.

17

Roll some scrap clay to a log 1cm diameter, 16cm long. Cover with strips of the same cane as you covered the body with, put through the pasta machine as before on PM2. Once covered, cut 2 x 4cm pieces and 2 x 4.5cm pieces. Round one end of each piece as shown on page 21. These are going to be the legs.

Making the knitted coat:

18

To make the knitting for the coat, first roll some yellow and purple clay (or whichever colours you want to use), around half a 56g block of each, to 1.5cm diameter, which is the thickness of the extruder, and 13cm long.

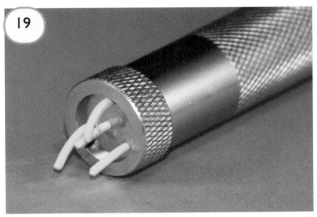

19

Put the extruder fitting with the 1.5mm round holes, and extrude both clays. If you don't have an extruder, roll the clay out to 1.5mm diameter logs.

20

Measure your dog from the middle of its chest to its tail, and add 3cm to the measurement. You need the extra length as when you 'knit' the clay, it will shorten. Cut the extruded, or rolled, clay to your measurement, and cut 28 lengths of each colour.

21

Take two lengths of the yellow clay and twist them, then take another two lengths and twist those as well, but in the opposite direction to the first two. So if you twist one to the left, the second will be to the right.

Next put the two twisted lengths together, trying to match the twists. They should look like a row of knitting.

Twist around 5 pairs of each colour, then put together as shown, alternating the colours to make a striped pattern.

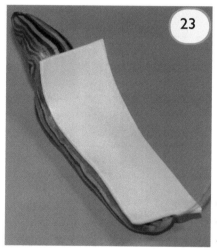

Roll some yellow clay, or any one of your two colours, on PM2 and cut a piece to the length of the middle of the chest to the tail, and as wide as you want the coat - measure this by working out where you want the knitted part of the coat to fall to one side of the dog, go over the top, and down to the same length the other side. If you are planning on adding a trim, cut the coat 6mm both sides shorter than the finished coat size. This is going to form the underside of the coat so it needs to be in one of the two coat colours.

Place the knitted clay on top of the piece of clay you measured for the coat, and cut to size.

Cut one end into a rounded shape, this will be the back of the coat, and make a cut from the middle of the other end to where the coat will sit at the base of the neck.

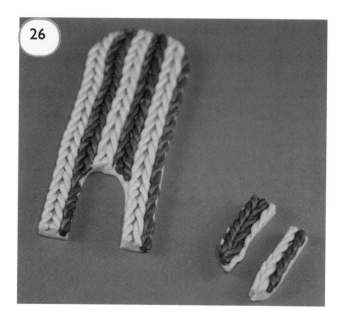

To make the coat fit round the dog's neck, make two cuts either side of the centre cut and make a rounded end. Keep fitting it on your dog and cutting until it fits nicely round his neck and to the front. Trim the front two pieces so they meet in the middle of the dog's chest. Put the coat to one side for now while you finish the legs.

Finishing the legs:

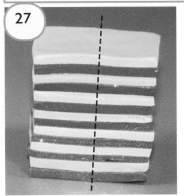

To make the striped edge for the legs (and the coat if you're making a trim), roll some clay of each colour on PM0 and cut 7 pieces of each of the two coat colours, 3cm x 2cm. Stack alternate colours as shown.

Cut the stack in half (the dotted line in previous picture) making two stacks of 1.5cm x 2cm, and stack these on top of each other, making a longer and thinner stack.

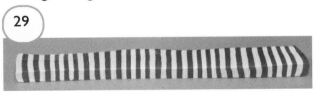

Cut two slices of the cane with a rigid blade, approximately 5mm thick. This is not very easy and as you can see in the picture, my cut was less than straight! However, don't worry as you're now going to put each slice through the pasta machine on PM0, with the stripes going downwards (vertical) - this will even it up and you will end up with a sheet of uniform thickness clay with the same width stripes. Put the two pieces together, making one wide sheet of vertical stripes, roll the join gently and cut along the long edge to make it straight. Lastly cut a piece off about 6mm wide. This is going to be the top of the legs, and the trim if you're having one.

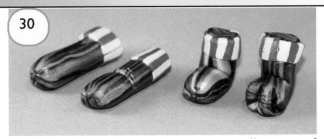

Take your four legs and wrap a small piece of the stripy edging round the top of each leg. With a thin knitting needle, make a crease across the clay, 1.5cm from the rounded end. Now carefully bend the leg to a right angle and finally make the feet by making three indentations in the end of each foot. The edge of your needle tool or cocktail stick works well for this, as does a rubber shaping tool, shown on the first page.

Once the legs and feet are made, match up the shorter ones (the front legs) and the longer ones (the back legs) into pairs, and press them together, with the feet pointing outwards at an angle as shown.

Put some Bake & Bond on the top of both pairs of legs and position the legs at the front and back of the dog. Gently press the body onto the legs to adhere, but not too heavily or you'll squash the legs.

33

To cover the tail use some of the body cane and wrap it round the tail, joining it to the body, and twisting it.

36

To make buttons to decorate the front of the coat, cut two 5mm circles in one of the two colours of the coat. Make four round holes using either a ball tool, needle tool or knitting needle, and lastly make two lines joining the four dots, or use thin rolls of clay to represent thread.

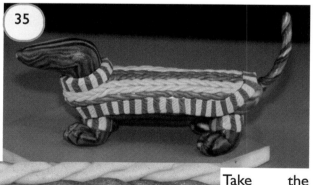

34

Take the coat and place it on the dog, making sure you are happy with the length and that it fits well on the dog. Finally press it securely to the dog.

35

Take the 6mm wide strip of stripy clay you cut earlier, lay it round the bottom edge of the coat and also round the neck, pressing gently onto the dog. I like to make diagonal marks to look like knitting.

Making the head:

37

Take some of the remaining slices of stripy cane and put lengthways through the pasta machine on PM1. Cut 4 x 15mm ovals, 3 x 12mm ovals, and 2 x 6mm circles. Roll a 5mm diameter ball of black clay for the nose. Also shown in the photo are 2 x 4mm black glass beads that will be the eyes.

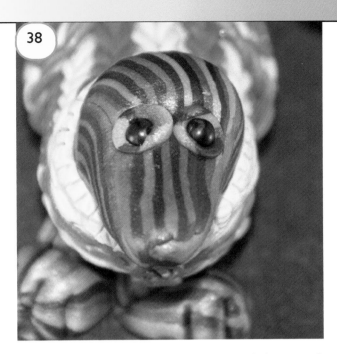

Take the two 6mm circles and slightly squash them with your finger before placing them 1cm apart on the head, at the point where the rounded part of the head dips down. Put a 4mm black glass bead in the middle of each circle.

For each oval, cut in half as shown, then make 4-5 marks, at a slight angle. Imagine leaf veins, make the two sets of marks pointing downwards and mirroring each other.

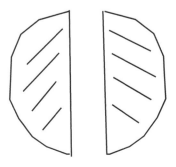

Take a pair of half ovals from the 12mm oval and place on top of each eye. Repeat with another pair, this time putting them underneath the eye - this is optional, I've done it with some of the dachshunds, but obviously not the one in this photo!

With the third 12mm oval pair, make a V shape, both pieces overlapping at the bottom, between the eyes.

Take the remaining 15mm oval pair and place either side of the nose to make a beard.

Now take the 3 x 15mm ovals pairs and starting nearest the eyes, place them either side of the nose as shown. I like to start off with the first pair touching in the middle, then place the other two a little apart. This gives a nicer line from the side.

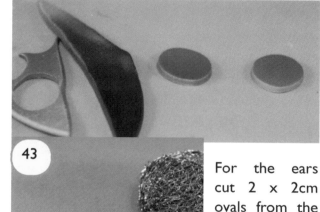

For the ears cut 2 x 2cm ovals from the off-cuts of clay and mould them into 'ear' shapes as shown. Texture with some rolled up foil and attach to each side of the head.

Darcy is now finished. Cure in a pre-heated oven at 130°C for 40 minutes. Varnish when cool if you want a shinier looking Darcy.

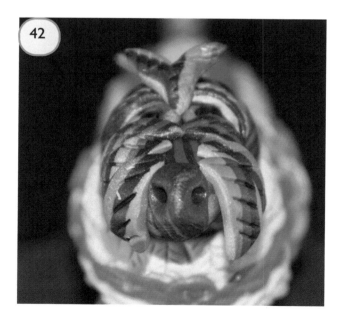

To make the nose, take the 5mm ball of black clay and mould into a triangular shape. Put on the face, making two holes for nostrils.

TOOLS & MATERIALS:

- Pasta machine
- Tissue blade
- Acrylic or metal clay roller
- Needle tool / cocktail stick
- Tile to work on
- Oven to cure clay in
- Good quality tin foil
- 1mm wire – 2 x 23cm and 2 x 14cm (I get it from the garden centre or DIY store)
- 10cm of 1mm brown wire for each reindeer
- Cyanoacrylate adhesive (also know as superglue)
- A ball tool approx 1cm diameter and another one around 1–2mm diameter
- Circle cutters 3cm. 7mm and 5mm (3/16") diameter
- 2 x 4mm black glass beads (2 per reindeer)
- Sticky tape (eg sellotape)
- Two pairs of flat nosed pliers
- Knitting needles – I use 7mm diameter and 4mm diameter ones
- Sculpey Bake & Bond clay adhesive
- Polymer clay varnish (optional). I use Darwi Vernis

Reindeer:

CLAY:

This is the amount for one reindeer:

- 1 x 56g brown clay – I use either Premo Sculpey bronze or Fimo Chocolate
- 1 x 56g Premo Sculpey Accents Copper
- 14g Black clay (1/4 of a 56g block)
- White clay (about the size of a pea)

Coat and boots/leg warmers:
(this is enough for two reindeers):

- 28g of red (1/2 a 56g block)
- 28g of green (1/2 a 56g block)
- 28g of gold (1/2 a 56g block)
- 28g of white (1/2 a 56g block)
- 14g of black (1/4 a 56g block)
- Pea size amount of orange clay for each carrot

Making the ears and tail:

1

I'm going to start with the ears and tail because it's easier to have the ears cured before putting them on the head. Roll out the brown clay and the copper clay each on PM0 and cut a 3cm circle of each. Following the Mo Clay method on page 20, make a blend.

2

Cut the blended clay into three equal peices as shown.

3

Stack the three pieces on top of each other.

4

Pinch one of the short ends then put through the pasta machine at PM0 short end first, to make a long ribbon, then again on PM2 & PM4.

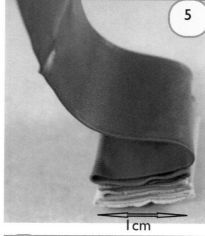

5

Now using a concertina or accordian fold (folding the clay backwards and forwards to build up into a block, called a plug) make a plug of clay in 1cm folds.

1cm

It doesn't matter whether you start with the light or dark end.

6

7

Lengthen the plug to 3cm wide then cut into 2 x 5mm and 1 x 2cm pieces.

8

Make the two smaller pieces into ears and the larger piece into a rugby ball shape for the tail. Make the lighter side the inside of the ears and score a line with a thin knitting needle down the middle. Cure the ears (not the tail) for 30 minutes at 130°C.

Making the reindeer body:

Take a piece of tin foil 30cm x 15cm and gently mould it into a rectangular shape. Gradually start to compress the foil into a flat rectangle with rounded edges, then make an indentation in the top and round the bottom corners to make a kidney bean shape. You are aiming to get a shape like this...........

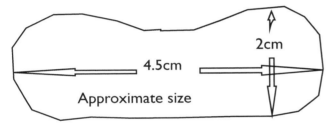

I use the work surface to help round the edges, and my clay roller to make the indentation on the top. Finally make two holes, first with the needle tool, and then with the 4mm diameter knitting needle as shown below.

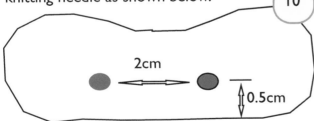

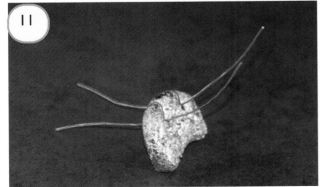

Take one of the 14cm pieces of wire, thread it through one of the holes, wrap it underneath the foil body and thread again through the hole, then tighten by pulling each end of the wire with a pair of pliers. Repeat with the other wire. I've coloured them blue and red so they show up in the photo.

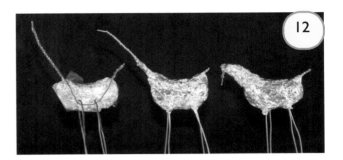

Left:
Now take one of the 23cm pieces of wire (the red one in the left picture above), place it underneath both leg wires (the blue ones), leaving just over 1cm at the tail end, and the longer piece at the front end which will become the head and neck. Using tape, secure the peice of wire to the foil body. Repeat with the other 23cm wire on the opposite side, then using pliers, twist the two peices together at each end.

Middle:
Using 2 x 5cm wide strips of foil, wrap them round the foil body and wire, this secures the leg wires and makes a smoother shape to put the clay on later.

Right:
Finally wrap another strip of foil round the neck to make it thicker. Leave 2.5cm bare wire for the head, then bend it to the position you want the head to face. Make sure you leave the tail wire free from foil as this will be covered by the tail you made earlier.

I've made this reindeer's head face downwards and slightly to the left.

Making the head:

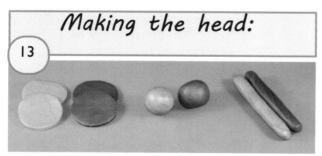

Cut 2 x 3cm circles of copper clay and 2 x 3cm circles of brown clay on PM0. Roll into two balls, then into logs 6cm long. Follow the Mo Clay method of making a blend on page 20.

The finished blend.

Using your clay blade cut one end at an angle. This is because, due to the mica pieces in the metalic clay, it is difficult to make the end of the cane blend in. By cutting it at an angle you are making the edge very thin so that when you roll it up there will be less of a mark.

Side view

Roll the piece up as shown, then smooth the join with a knitting needle.

Next, using the technique shown on page 21, make each end of the reindeer head rounded. You are aiming to pull the edges of the ends into the middle and smoothing down. Finally mould the head into a shape larger at the light coloured end, and 4cm long.

Making up the body:

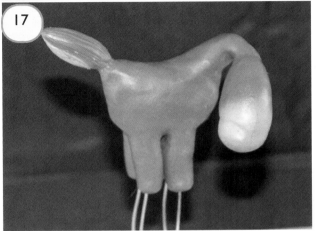

Roll out the brown clay on PM2 and cover the body. Add more brown clay to the neck to make it thicker.

For the legs, roll out brown clay on PM0 and cut 4 x 3cm circles. Roll each circle into a ball then a log 2cm long. Thread onto the legs and join to the body by smoothing the join with a knitting needle.

Push the head on, smoothing the join, and do the same for the tail, making sure that the light part is underneath.

I like to make stripes in the tail to show hair by using a thin knitting needle. This is optional.

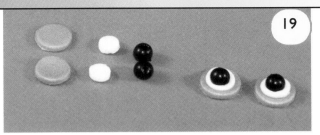

For the eyes cut:
2 x 7mm circles in copper, and
2 x 5mm (3/16") circles in white
both on PM4.

Put the white circle on top of the copper circle and place the 6mm black glass bead in the middle.

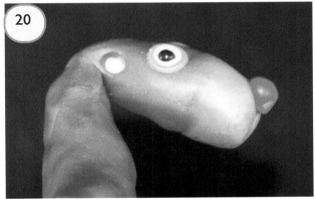

Place the eyes around 2/3rds of the way from the bottom of the reindeer head towards the top.

Roll a pea size ball of red clay and place it on the head for a nose. You can put two nostril holes in if liked.

Make two holes with the 7mm diameter knitting needle, put some Bake & Bond in the

hole and push in the ears.
If you haven't cured the ears you won't need the Bake & Bond.

For the mouth make a hole using the 4mm needle, then make a line from mouth to nose.

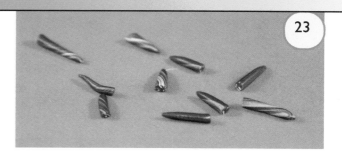

To make the mane, twist some brown and copper clay together, roll into a log roughly 3mm diameter and cut off 1cm pieces.

Make one end of each of the pieces pointed. You will need around 12-14 pieces.

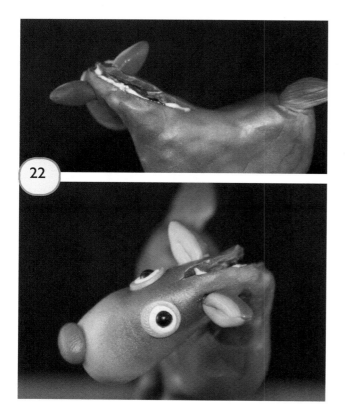

To make the mane, first make a cut, appoximately 5mm deep, in the neck starting from between the ears down to just in front of his back. Use a craft knife for this cut. Put some Bake & Bond in the cut.

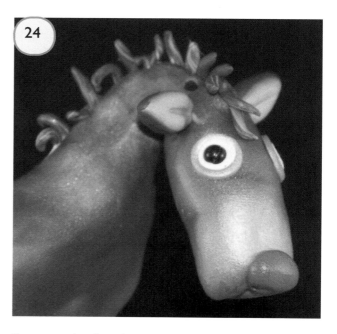

Start at the head end and insert the pieces of mane in, pointed end uppermost, one at a time. Take your time putting each piece in and pushing it up to the previous one before continuing. Once completed push the two sides of the neck together, closing the cut. Make two holes just behind the ears with 4mm diameter knitting needle, this is to insert the antlers once the reindeer is finished. **Important: Read steps 25 & 26 before curing.** You are now ready to cure the reindeer in the oven for 40 minutes at 130°C.

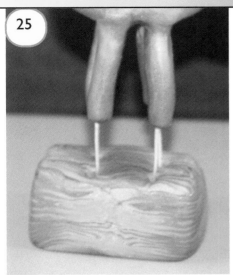

25

To keep the reindeer standing upright during curing, I like to shape some scrap clay into a block, make four holes in it and insert the four reindeer leg wires in the holes. I then put the whole thing in a cardboard box (I used the box that coffee pods come in), put scrunched up kitchen roll round the whole reindeer to protect it, and cure in the oven. The block can then be used many times over.

26

These are the handy coffee pod boxes that I use to cure the reindeer in; however, any cardboard boxes would do, and as long as you protected the reindeer, you could get away without the clay block if necessary. This picture shows the finished reindeer, but I use them at this first stage as well.

However you choose to cure your reindeer, make sure that they can't fall over. It's so disheartening when you spend ages on your reindeer, put it in the oven, then bring it out 30 minutes later minus an ear or two and with half its mane missing. Trust me, I've done it with several ponies and reindeer!

Making the canes for the coat and boots or leg warmers:

Star cane:

27

Roll out some red clay on PM0 and cut 4 x 3cm diameter circles. Roll the circles together and form into a cube.

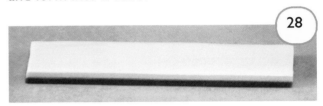

28

Roll some white clay on PM2 and cut a rectangle, 2cm x 8cm. Roll gold clay on PMO, place the white rectangle on the sheet of gold clay and cut to the same size.

29

Pinch one of the short ends, and put through the pasta machine on PM0, pinched short end first.

131

30

Put through the pasta machine again, this time on PM2. You are going to use this to make the star in the cane.

31

With the non-sharp edge of your clay blade, make four marks in the cube. Two diagonally and two across the middle as shown by the dashed lines.

It's really important that your cuts are straight, so it's also a good idea to make marks down the edges of the cube as well, as shown in the thin black lines.

When you make the cuts, make sure that the blade follows the lines on the side of the cube, it keeps it straight.

32

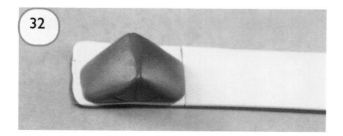

Cut the cube in half diagonally and place on the white/gold strip. Cut round the red clay.

33

Place the red clay with it's side of white/gold back with the other piece of red clay. You can see that the red clay I've used is a little soft and is squashing down. I probably used Premo which should have been leached first. However, the cane still came out alright, so don't worry too much if this happens.

34

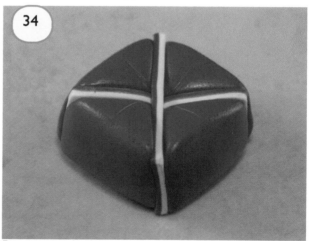

Repeat with the other diagonal cut.

35

For the two remaining cuts you are going to do the same as before, but leave a little gap between the white/gold strip and the edge of the cube. This is so the star has different length lines in it and makes a more interesting design when finished.

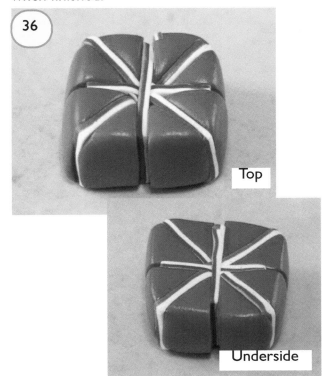

Top

Underside

This is the finished star. You will notice that the red clay was quite soft so it's sunk a little when cut. The bottom photo shows the underneath of the cube, all the lines meet in the middle. This will mean that the stars will remain the same all the way through and not become distorted.

Now start lengthening the cube by pressing gently in the middle of the sides and pulling carefully. Then gently roll on all sides until 3cm wide.

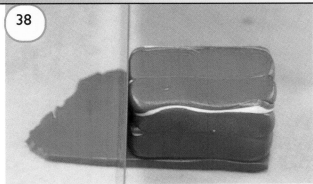

When it's reached 3cm, roll some red clay on PM0 and lay the cane on it, cutting to size. You do this on only one side. This is to create a gap between the stars in the finished cane.

Lengthen to 14cm - I like to do this using my clay roller on each side then pulling gently. Cut off the distorted ends and lengthen again to 14cm.

Cut into 7 x 2cm pieces. When you look at each piece you will notice that one side of the star has an extra strip of red on it. It is very important that when you put the 7 pieces together, that the sides with the extra red clay on them are all in the same position, eg to the left or right.

This is so that the line of stars will not be touching each other and they will stand out more.

Diamond cane:

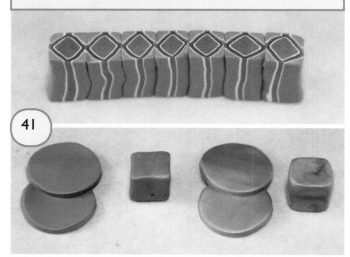

Roll green and gold clay on PM0 and cut 2 x 3cm circles of both. Roll the 2 green circles into a ball, then a cube. Repeat with the gold clay.

Roll some white clay on PM6 and cover both cubes. Place the cube on the white clay and cut it to the width of the cube. Cut a straight line behind the cube as well.

Roll the cube along the white clay, then using your tissue blade, cut off the excess clay.

Roll out some black clay on PM6 and cover the gold cube. Roll out some red clay on PM2 and cover the green cube. The green cube needs to be slightly larger than the gold one which is why the red clay is thicker. Cut the green centred cube into quarters by making two diagonal cuts from corner to corner, as shown by the dotted lines.

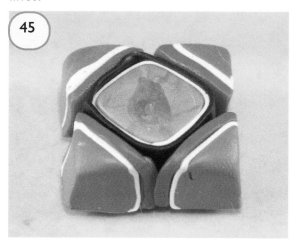

Place the four pieces round the gold cube as shown, making a square shape.

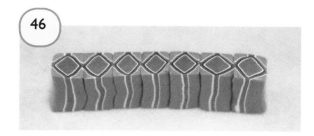

Lengthen the cane to 14cm, cut off the distorted ends and lengthen again to 14cm. Cut into 7 x 2cm pieces and put together in a line. This is now ready to use, put to one side to use later.

Stripy:

This isn't a cane as such, but a sheet of stripy clay that can be cut into strips and added in the coat/boot/leg warmer design.

Roll gold clay on PM0 and cut four squares, 2cm x 2cm.

Roll white clay on PM4 and lay each gold square on it, cutting round the squares.

Continue to build up the squares in the same was as you did with the white clay. Next layer is green, PM0. Now, taking the strip of white/gold clay left over from the star cane, use that to make the next layer. You may need to make it a little thinner if it isn't long enough. The final two layers are red PM0 and black PM6.

Stack the four squares on top of each other as shown, keep the gold on the top of each.

George my cat wanted to get in on the photograph! One of the perils of working on the kitchen table!

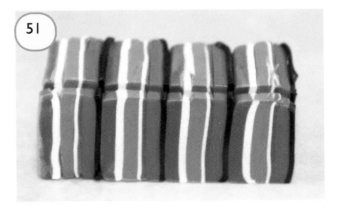

Put the stack on its side and cut a couple of 3mm slices.

135

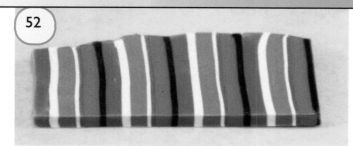

Put the slices through the pasta machine on PM0 first, then again on PM2, with the stripes vertical. It is now ready to use. Put to one side.

Houndstooth cane:

This is not my cane design, I found it on the Internet on several sites and couldn't find the original artist to credit. It is a wonderfully simple yet effective design.

Roll green and white clay out on PM0 and cut four x 3cm circles of each colour. The rest of the photos are going to show the cane in brown as the green was a little soft and didn't photograph well.

Pod the kitten now wants to be in the photo!

Make 2 brown stacks and 2 white stacks, each containing 2 circles of clay.

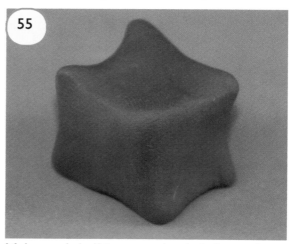

Make each ball into a cube. It helps to have really sharp corners and I find the easiest way to get this is to pinch each of the 8 corners as shown. Then use your clay roller to smooth the sides.

The four cubes.

Once you have four cubes, take one brown and one white and put three cuts in each: one diagonally from corner to corner, then one either side of the first cut, half way between the first cut and the corner. This leaves you with two uncut cubes and two cut ones.

Now swap two of the pieces in each cube to make two stripy cubes.

Put the four cubes together as shown.

Lengthen the cane to 14cm, cut off any distorted ends and lengthen again to 14cm. Cut into four equal pieces.

Put the four pieces together, making sure that they are all facing the same way. The way I do it is to look at the bits that look like the end of a ribbon.....

and make sure they all match direction.
Lengthen the cane again to 14cm, and cut into four again. When you've put them together your cane is ready.

The finished cane, although yours will be in green!

Swirly cane:

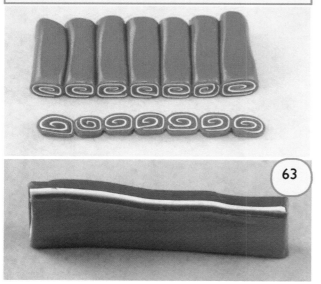

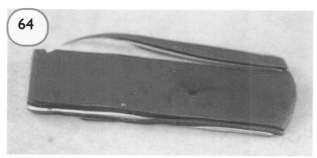

Roll some red clay on PM0 and cut a rectangle 6cm x 3cm

Roll white clay on PM4, put the red rectangle on top of the white and cut round. Finally roll some gold clay on PM2 and put the rectangle on it, cutting round again, making a three layered rectangle.

With your clay roller, make the rectangle gradually thinner, you are looking for this shape...

Side view

Don't worry about the clay becoming wider as you make it thinner, just get the slope first.
Once done, take your tissue blade and cut the rectangle to the 3cm width all the way down as shown in the picture.

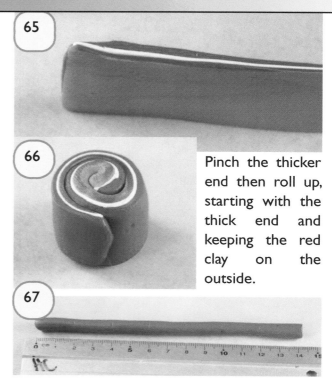

Pinch the thicker end then roll up, starting with the thick end and keeping the red clay on the outside.

Lengthen the cane to 14cm, cut off the distorted ends and lengthen again to 14cm. Cut into 7 x 2cm pieces.

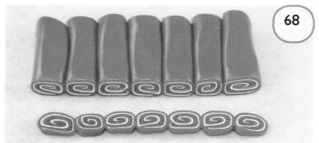

Put the 7 pieces next to each other, making sure they are all facing the same way ie the 'tails' are all either facing left or right.

The finished canes.

Making the leg warmers:

For your reindeer, decide whether you want to make leg warmers or boots. These are the instructions for leg warmers, boots are next.

Roll scrap clay on PM0 and cut a 3cm circle. Roll this into a ball and then a 2cm log. Make four.

To cover the leg warmers, first wrap thin strips of your canes round the log, you can use whichever canes you like and in whatever order. Once covered, roll gently to join all the canes.

Lastly, using a 1cm diameter ball tool, make a convex shape in each end of the leg warmer as shown.
Make sure you've covered the edge with canes so that when the leg warmer attaches to the leg and hoof, the scrap clay doesn't show.

For each hoof roll black clay on PM0 and cut a 3cm circle. Roll into a ball, then, leaving the ball on the work surface, twist it round so that the base goes flat and the top is a dome shape. Finally make an indentation in the base one side with the 4mm needle.

Cut the leg wire to size. Lay the leg warmer and the hoof next to the end of the leg and cut the wire around 7mm shorter than the end of the hoof. This allows for compression when attaching the leg and hoof.

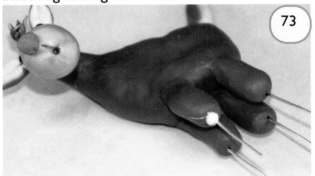

Put a blob of polymer clay glue such as Bake & Bond onto the underneath of the reindeer leg.

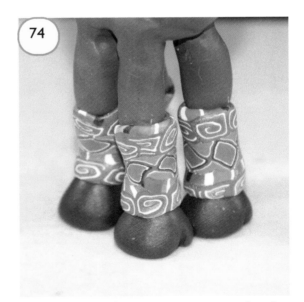

Thread each leg warmer onto the leg wire followed by a hoof. Make sure the hooves are facing the right way, the cloven indented part should be at the front.

Making the boots :

Roll scrap clay on PM0 and cut 2 x 3cm circles. Roll these into a ball and then a 4cm log. Make four.

For the boots, cover the 4cm log with cane slices, roll to join the slices, then round the end that is going to be the toe of the boot (as shown on page 21).

On the other end use the 1cm ball tool to make a convex indentation as shown on the leg warmer. The boot will be around 5cm once covered. Make a bend 2cm from the toe end and your boot is completed.

Lay the boot next to the end of the leg and cut the leg wire 7mm from the end of the boot.

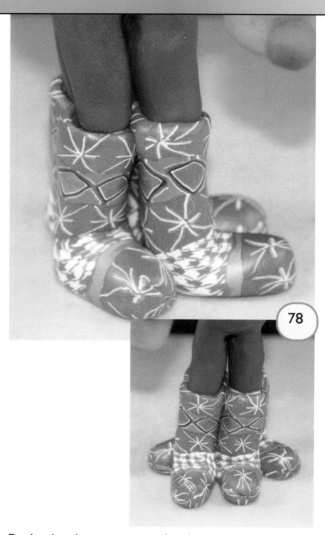

Push the boots onto the leg wire. As I have made this reindeer's legs quite close togther, the back boots need to stick out to the side.

Boots and leg warmers in place!

Making the coat:

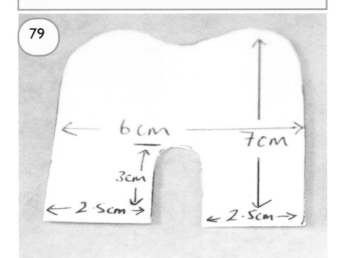

Make a paper or cardboard template of a coat, dimensions shown above. This gives a pattern for a coat which you can adapt to fit.

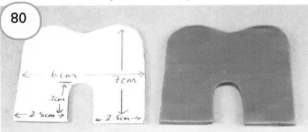

Roll out some clay in a colour that goes with your canes as a little of the underside of the coat will show. Roll the clay out on PM2 and cut to the size of your pattern.

Place the coat on your reindeer and trim accordingly. You might find that the coat needs to be shortened, or the front cut so it fits, as shown in the bottom picture.

Take into consideration whether you're going to have binding on the coat or not; if you're adding binding, cut the coat around 3mm shorter each side. You may want to put a trim on it; again, work out the depth of trim, and take that measurement off the length.

Take the coat off the reindeer to continue.

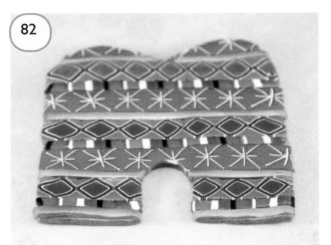

Cut thin strips off your canes and cover the coat completely.

In order to join the cane slices and make a nice smooth coat, you need to burnish it. Burnishing it means polishing it, making the surface smooth and getting rid of any uneven parts.

To burnish it I use layout paper and a soapstone, but you can use greaseproof paper and a smooth stone or bone folder tool, or even your fingers if you prefer. You can buy layout paper in art supplies, and soapstones are quite cheap on the Internet. Lay the paper over your reindeer coat and gently rub the soapstone in curcular movements over the paper. Keep checking the clay to see when the whole piece is smooth and the clay pieces have joined.

Fit the coat on your reindeer to make sure it still fits. If it's too large, cut it to size. If it's too small you could consider putting a thick binding on it, or make up a trim all the way round.

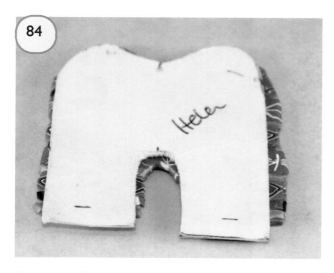

Once you've burnished the coat it will have stretched. Put the pattern back on it and cut again to size. I use a craft knife to cut the shaped parts and a tissue blade for the straight edges.

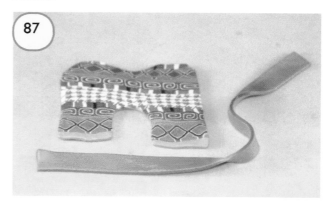

You can either leave your coat as it is, or put a binding on it. To make the binding, roll some clay the colour you want on PM3, and cut a strip 1cm wide.

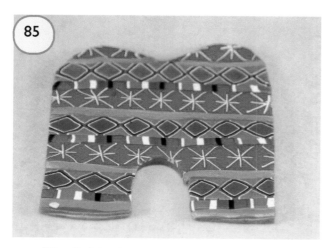

The finished coat.

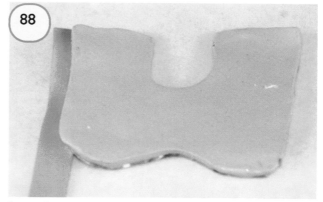

Lay the coat, top side facing down, on the binding, leaving around half the width showing. Don't try and do this part all the way round, just do one edge.

89

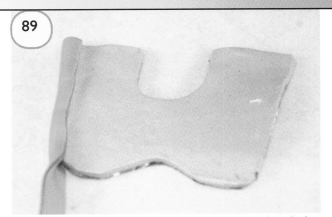

Fold over the clay before going on to bind the next part.

90

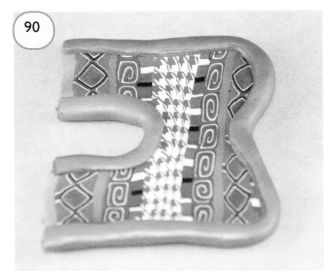

Leave the two front edges to last.

91

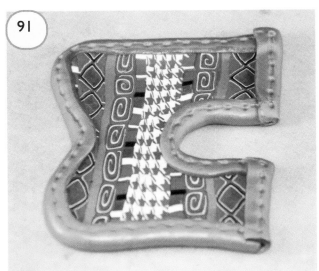

Finally bind the two front edges, and using a small ball tool, needle tool or cocktail stick,

make marks that look like stitching. Do this by making a hole, then dragging the tool or stick lightly across the clay to the next hole.

The two completed coats, one bound and one not.

92

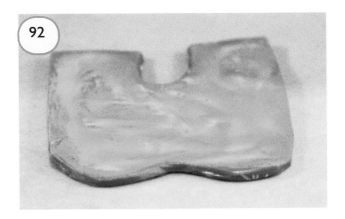

When you're ready to attach the coat to your reindeer, first cover the back of the coat with a thin layer of polymer clay glue such as Bake & Bond.

Fit onto the reindeer, gently pressing down at the top and front but leaving the bottom of the coat hanging naturally.

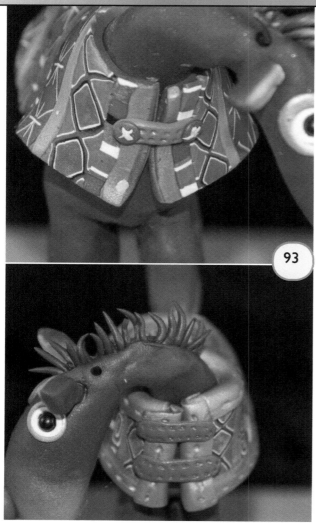

93

95

Cure your reindeer at 130° C for 30 minutes, again in the coffee pod box to protect it!

Making the antlers :

For each antler, take the 1mm wire and cut 5cm. Fold at 2cm.

Using the flat nosed pliers, pinch the bend tightly.

Next, using the round nose pliers, bend the shorter wire round one one of the round jaws, bending it away from the other piece of wire. Repeat with the longer piece.

Note that they are both curled the same way. Make two of these for each reindeer. Glue them into the two holes behind the ears.

You've now finished your first reindeer - have fun adding to the herd with your own designs!

Make a fastening for the front of the coat. In the top picture I've made one strap and put two clay buttons on it. The bottom picture has two straps.

94

144

Making carrots:

Roll a ball of orange clay the size of a small pea, lengthen it to around 2cm, making it larger one end and pointed the other. Finally put a hole in the middle of the larger end with the 4mm knitting needle.

Roll some green clay 2mm thick and cut 3 x 8mm pieces, point one end and join the pieces together at the other end. Poke the green clay stalks into the end of the carrot, and finally make lines round the carrot with the back of your tissue blade. Cure 20 minutes at 130° C.

My clay group of friends tested out the tutorial. Left to right:
Ruth's, Belinda's, Linda's and Tracy's reindeers'.

Kaleidoscope Cane:
and some things to make with it.

Apologies, I made this cane a while ago and used inches in all the measurements. Ever since I attended a workshop with Carol Simmons I tend to make large canes in inches.

TOOLS & MATERIALS:

- Pasta machine
- Tissue blade
- Acrylic or metal clay roller
- Needle tool / cocktail stick
- Tile to work on
- Oven to cure clay in
- Ruler
- Standard playing card, or a piece of card 9cm x 6cm

These colours are for the green/yellow cane:

Fimo Professional:
- 1.5oz Yellow
- 1.5oz Purple
- 1.5oz True Green
- 1.5oz Black
- 5oz White
- A hazelnut size of dark brown

For the caterpillar:
- Circle cutter 2cm diameter
- Scrap clay
- 2 x 3mm black glass beads
- 6cm of thin wire
- Polymer clay varnish. I use Darwi Vernis (optional)

CLAY:

These colours are for the blue/yellow cane:

Fimo Professional:
- 1.5oz Lemon Yellow
- 1.5oz Violet
- 1.5oz Ultramarine
- 1.5oz Black
- 5oz White

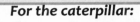

Cane by Ruth Peck

Making the blends:

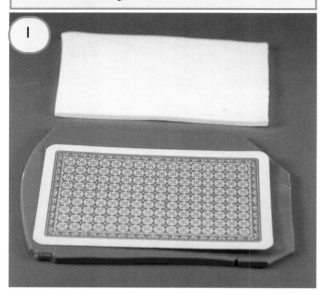

Roll some white clay and some true green clay on PM0 and cut round a standard playing card, or piece of card 9cm x 6cm.

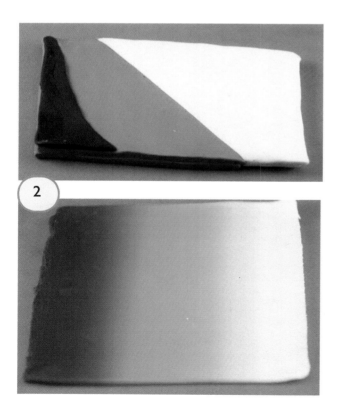

Following steps 1 to 4 on page 18, make a skinner blend.

Repeat with the purple and yellow, using black to darken the purple and brown to darken the yellow. Cut each blend in half as shown.

Striped Bulls Eye Cane:

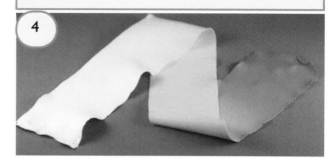

Take one of the pieces of yellow blend and put it through lengthways through the pasta machine on PM0 - white end pointing downwards. Put the pasta machine on PM2 and put through again. Repeat on PM4, and finally PM6. You will end up with a long thin piece of clay.

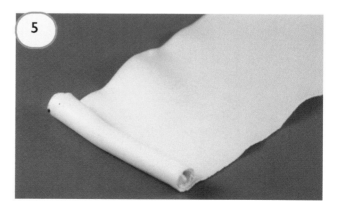

Following the instructions on page 22, roll up the clay from the white end.

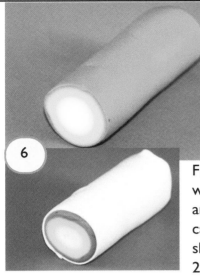

You now have a bulls eye cane with the dark yellow on the outside.

Finally roll some white clay on PM7 and cover the cane - this is shown on page 22.

Roll some black and white clay on PM1 and cut two pieces of each, 1.5" x 3".

Using your blade, cut 8 of the 3mm wide slices off the black and place next to each other. Roll

gently with your roller to join, then carefully place the stripes round the bulls eye cane. You may need to add another slice or take some away to make it fit.

Stack the pieces of clay, alternating black and white, and mark out 3mm as shown. Yes, hope you've noticed that I'm doing most of the canes in inches, then I sneak a few millimetres in!

Mark the cane from the short end. I used a Marxit tool (shown on the left), but you can easily measure and mark it using a ruler.

Cover the cane in thin white - rolled on PM7, then roll to 3", cut off the distorted ends and roll again to 3". Cut in half and put one half to the side. Roll the remaining piece to 3" and cut in half. You now have three pieces of the striped bulls eye cane.

Criss-cross Cane:

Take the remaining strip of blended yellow clay and cut in half lengthways as shown.

Lengthen each piece as you did in step 4. You are now going to make each piece into a 'plug' of clay. This is a useful technique that forms the basis of many canes.

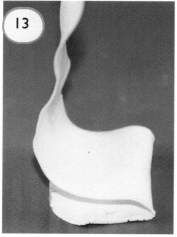

Holding the strip of clay vertically, fold it in 1" wide folds, carefully pressing down each fold until all the clay is used.

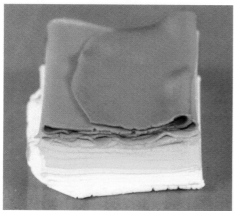

The completed plug of clay.

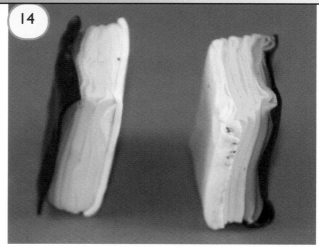

Roll each plug until they both measure 1.5" x 1", then roll some white clay on PM4 and cover the white side of ONE piece. Finally roll some black clay on PM4 and cover BOTH dark sides.

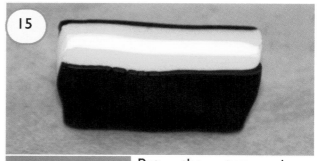

Put the two pieces together, white sides together, then gently roll the clay, turning it over after each roll until it measures 2.5" long.
Put it through the pasta machine on PM0 lengthways.

Finally trim off the edges which will have become distorted and lost some of the black

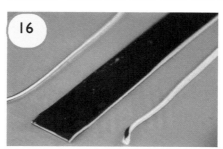

clay. Your piece is now ready to add to the next piece of the criss-cross cane.

17

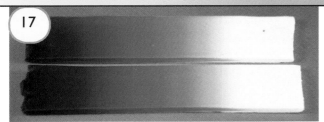

Take one of the purple pieces and cut in half lengthways. Roll each piece through the pasta maching on PM1, then stack one on top of the other, and put through the pasta machine again on PM1.

18

Continue to make the strip longer and thinner as in step 4, then roll up, light side first into a bulls eye cane.

19

Make a cut approximately a third of the way across the cane.

20

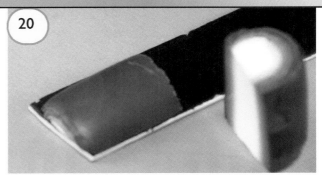

Lay the smaller piece cut side down on the strip of yellow/black clay that you've just made. Cut it to fit the purple piece. Put it back, and you have your first cut.

Do three more cuts, following the steps in the next three photographs.

21

The third cane is one taught to me by Carol Simmons and she gave me permission to pass it on to others.

For this cane you are going to use two bulls eye canes, made from the remaining purple piece and one of the green pieces. Following steps 4 and 5, roll up the purple strip with the darker colour inside, and the green strip with the white inside.

Your cane is now ready to lengthen. Roll to 3", cut off the distorted ends and roll to 3" again. Cut in half; your criss-cross cane is now completed.

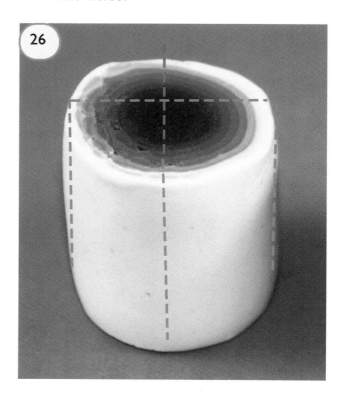

Cut each cane into four as shown.

152

You now have 8 segments.

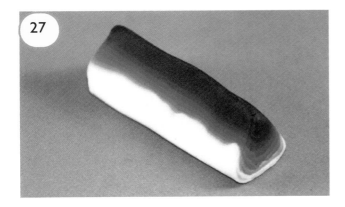

Take one of the purple segments and carefully pull the white clay layer part-way up the sides. Make the top - the dark part - into a sharp point. Repeat with the other three segments.

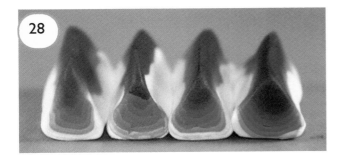

Lay the four purple segments side by side as shown, and touching.

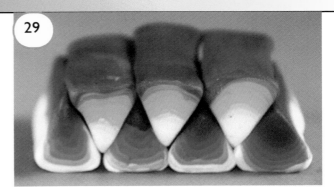

Make the white ends of the green segments pointed and place three in between the purple segments.

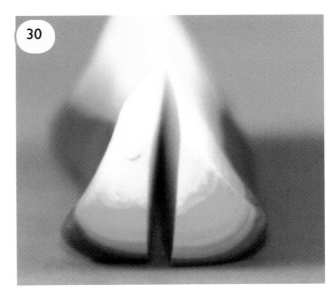

Take the fourth green segment and cut in half as shown.

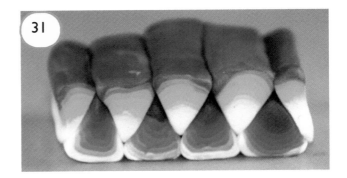

Place the two half segments at either end of the cane.

153

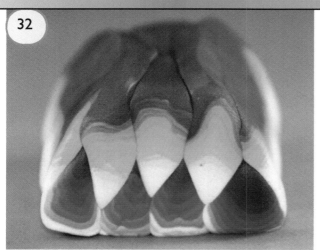

Start gently pressing the green end inwards, making a point. You will end up with a triangular shaped cane. Lengthen the cane to 4", cut off the distorted ends and roll again to 4". Cut off 1.5" and put both pieces aside.

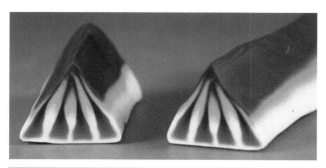

Blended Jelly Roll Cane:

For the forth cane, take the remaining piece of green blended clay, cut in half, place one piece on top of the other and roll gently to adhere. Roll some white clay on PM3 and lay the green clay piece on top.

Cut round it, trimming the white to the same size. Repeat with black clay, again rolled on PM3.

With your roller, gently roll the white end to make a graduated point.

Start rolling from the white end, with the black clay on the outside.

When you're nearly at the end, slightly flatten the darker end, then complete rolling.

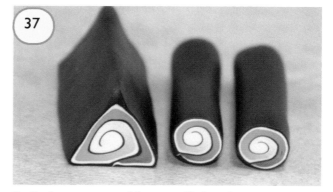

Roll the cane to 3", cut off the distorted ends and roll again to 3". Cut off 1.5" and make it into a triangular shape (the cane on the left). Roll the remaining piece to 3" and cut in half. You now have three pieces of blended jelly roll cane; put to one side.

Ladder Cane:

I can't remember where I learnt this cane from, possibly in a Donna Kato tutorial, but not sure, and I can't find it. Anyway, it's a very useful little cane to have in your toolkit as it brings a distinctive pattern to many canes, and is so easy to make.

For cane five, cut another 8 slices of the striped block used in the striped bulls eye cane, lay them side by side and gently roll to adhere. Roll some yellow clay on PM3 and put the stripes on top of it. Cut the yellow to size.

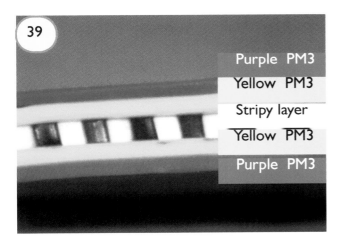

Purple PM3
Yellow PM3
Stripy layer
Yellow PM3
Purple PM3

Cover the other side of the stripy cane with yellow, again on PM3. Repeat with purple, again on PM3, covering both sides on top of the yellow.

Now roll the clay sheet with your roller <u>in the direction of the stripes, NOT across them</u>. This is very important as you want the stripes to stay the same width, not be wider.

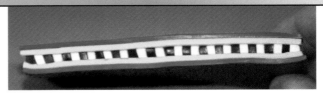

Turn the clay over after each roll, and continue until it measures 3". Straighten the edges and roll again to 3". Cut in half as shown above.

Layered Bulls Eye Cane:

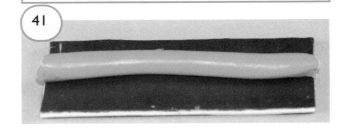

This last cane uses up the last bits of clay. Roll a log of green clay that fits in the remaining piece of yellow/black clay left over from the criss-cross cane.

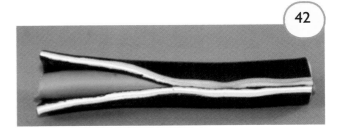

Wrap the yellow/black clay round the green log, then roll some while clay on PM7 (or as thin as you can make it) and cover the cane, following the steps on page 22. Repeat with a layer of purple on PM4, then finally a layer of green on PM2.

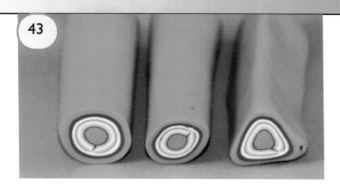

Roll to 3", cut off distorted ends and roll to 3" again. Cut in half, and put one piece to one side. Roll the remaining piece to 3" and cut in half. Make one half into a triangle and leave the other as a round cane.

Making the Cane - putting it all together:

These are the canes used for the kaleidoscope cane all 1.5" long. 2 x stripy bulls eye (1 large, 1 smaller diameter), 1 x sharks tooth, 1 x criss-cross, 2 x blended jelly roll (1 smaller circle and 1 larger triangle), 2 x layered bulls eye (1 larger circle and 1 smaller triangle), 1 x piece of ladder cane.

These are the canes that you will have left over; they can be used in so many ways!

Cut a 2mm slice off each of the nine canes you are using to make the kaleidoscope cane.

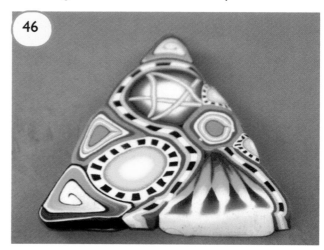

This is my absolute favourite part of making a complex cane - designing it. I learnt this way of designing a complex cane from Carol Simmons in her Master Cane workshop. If you ever get the opportunity to go to this workshop, don't hesitate, I learnt so much in it. Take your 2mm slices and arrange them into a triangle, with roughly equal lengthed sides. Take your time over this; you can change the shape of any cane, cut it, shorten it, anything actually to make your design. You will notice that I cut the ladder cane into two pieces, cut the smaller stripy bulls eye cane in half, and made the smaller jelly roll into a triangle. Bear in mind that the design you make will be repeated, so if you put for example a circle next to the edge, if those edges touch you will have two circles next to each other. Once you're happy with the design, replicate it with the canes.

These are two other designs you can make for this tutorial which will hopefully help you design yours. However, feel free to put the canes in whatever design you like; these are just examples.

Put the canes together carefully, making sure that every cane is in the same position all the way along, so that when you turn the cane over, one end is the same as the other.

Once your cane is made it's time to lengthen it. Take your time over this, pressing the cane from the middle outwards, constantly checking that the ends are not distorting any more than necessary. Although it's unlikely that that you won't have any distortion, by constantly checking and adjusting the ends as much as possible, it will limit the wastage. The way I lengthen it is to press all the way along from the middle to the outside, gently pulling, and smoothing the edges afterwards. However, everyone has their own way of doing it, so experiment and do whatever works best for you.

Continue lengthening the cane until it measures 7.5", cut off the distorted ends and lengthen again to 7.5". You may have to cut off distorted ends again, if so, just cut them off and lengthen again to 7.5". You want to end up

with 7.5" of good cane. Finally cut the cane into 6 pieces, each one 1.25" long. Measure these as it's very important that they are all exactly the same.

Cut 1 x 2mm slice off each piece. These are going to be used to work out how you're going to put your cane together. The following three pictures show the three different ways my cane could be made, each one having a different corner in the middle.

Don't worry that they look a little uneven, 2mm slices are easy to distort, what you want to look at is the pattern.

Which one has the most pleasing design?

Personally I liked the middle one best so made my final cane in that pattern. Put the six pieces together very carefully, making sure that they match all the way along, constantly checking that each piece is in exactly the same place from one end to the other.

The bottom picture is a second cane I made, following the same method, but it came out slightly differently. Make sure you press the finished cane together firmly to get rid of any gaps inside.

The kaleidoscope cane makes a lovely turtle shell!

Making a caterpillar:

The spare canes can be used to make a caterpillar. This can be hooked over a vase or used as an ornament.

Roll some scrap clay on PM0 and cut a 2cm circle, then roll it into a ball. Make 12 in total.

158

For the head roll one and a half circles of clay, this makes the head slightly larger.

The finished balls ready to be covered with the cane slices.

To cover the scrap clay ball, cut thin slices of one of the canes. You might want to make the cane a little smaller first as it makes it easier to fit the slices on the ball.

Once the ball is covered, carefully pinch the edges of the slices together so that the clay covers any gaps, hiding the scrap clay. It is important to do this step before you roll the ball smooth.

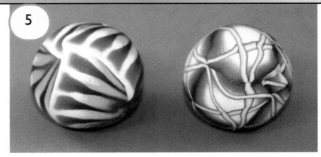

Finally, once you've covered any scrap clay, roll the ball in the palms of your hands to smooth the joins and make it round. I like to roll a few times clockwise, then a few times anti-clockwise, this helps the ball become round and not end up like a rugby ball!

Cover the 12 smaller balls with the cane slices. I like to make two of each pattern. Cover the larger 'head' ball with one of the plain colours, I've used purple.

Slightly flatten each ball as shown. The part that will be seen is the outside edge, so try to flatten them with this in mind.

Look at the colours and put the different balls into a pleasing pattern.

8

Following the pattern you've just made, push the flattened balls together, with the head at the front. I like to shape the last ball into a cone shape.

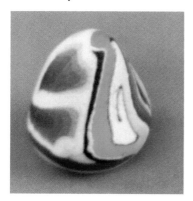

The cone shaped ball.

9

Mould the caterpillar into the shape above.

10

To make the head, cut some circles of the stripy bulls eye cane and put on the head, inserting a 3mm black glass beads in the centre of each for eyes. Roll a small ball of clay for the nose and place on the front.

11

Make a little mark under the nose to look like a mouth.

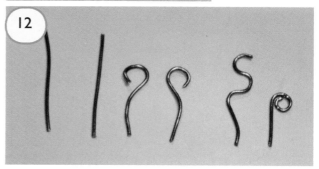

12

For the antennae cut 2 x 3cm pieces of thin wire, then shape them any way you like, I've shown some examples above.

13

Push the antennae into the top of the head. You can now either leave your caterpillar as it is, or make it so it can hook on the side of a vase.

Making the caterpillar so it can hook over a vase:

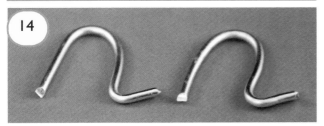

Cut some soft wire, around 2mm diameter, to 5cm. Cut two.

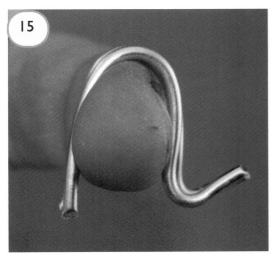

To get the distinct shape, wrap both pieces at the same time over your finger (I've shown only one). Bending the two together ensures that you get identical shapes. Then, while the wires are still on your finger, take some pliers and bend the end, around 1cm upwards.

With a small knitting needle, or even the wire you made the two hooks from, make two holes underneath the caterpillar on the 2nd segment from the head.

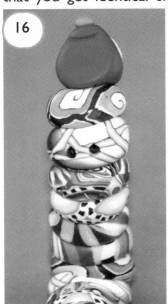

Cure the caterpillar at 130°C for 30 minutes. Varnish when cool - optional. To hang the caperpillar over a vase, push the short bent ends of the hooks in the holes underneath the caterpillar and hook onto the vase.

Making use of the scraps:

They're such lovely canes, that it seems a pity to turn the scrap bits into mud coloured clay. This is a technique that I've seen many times on the Internet, but I learnt it from Birdy Heywood, and continue to be amazed at some of the results of this technique.

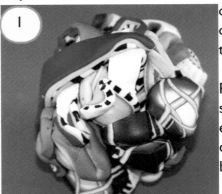

Roll the scrap clay ends and off-cuts into a ball.

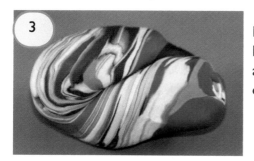

Roll the ball into a log, then twist it.

Fold the log in half and give it one twist.

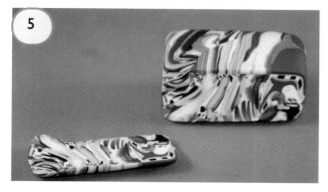

Make the clay into a cube. The width of the final pattern will be twice the height of the cube, so take this into account when deciding what shape to make it.

With a sharp clay blade, cut a piece off the cube in order to straighten up the front edge.

Cut the cube into even slices, the width doesn't really matter, as long as they're all the same.

Take the first two slices and lay them next to each other, the sides uppermost being next to each other (touching). In this way their pattern is a mirror image. Hold them up, one in each hand, and press them together, matching the pattern exactly. It is easier doing this in the air as if the slices are different widths it will not be possible on the work surface.

Lay the joined piece down, mirrored pattern downwards on the work surface.

If your two slices are uneven in width, this is your time to add some more clay to the thinner one. Push them together firmly to join the seam. Lift them carefully up and turn them over to see the finished pattern.

The resulting mirror-image piece can be made into many other projects. Be careful not to over-touch or burnish the pattern as it is only very thin and can easily distort or smudge.

The following three pictures are made from the scrap from one kaleidoscope cane.

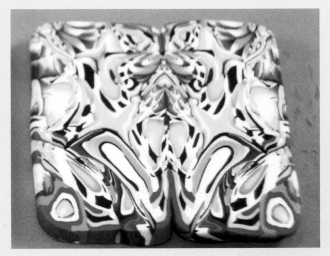

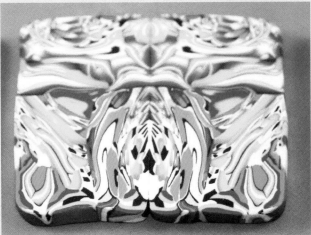

So many ways to use the canes:

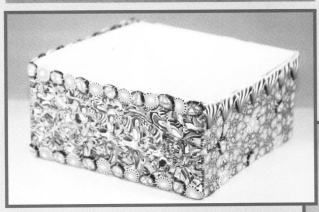

I covered a cardboard box with slices of the canes, and also slices of the scrap clay. It sits on my window sill and holds the dog's medication!!

Suppliers:

Not an extensive list, but the ones that I use.

ClayAround
www.clayaround.com
A real treasure trove of clay goodies for all your claying needs, with exceptional customer service from Penny Vingoe. Categories include:

- Accessories
- Bezel settings
- Clay cutting blades
- Decorating surfaces
- Embossing & distressing
- Fat Daddio cutters
- Gilders wax
- Inka Gold
- Kemper cutters
- Liquid & special clay
- Mica powder
- Pan pastels
- Premo clay
- Souffle clay
- Alcohol inks
- Books
- Crafting tools
- Fimo Clay
- Foils
- Heat set paints
- Kato clay
- Kor tools
- Melanie Muir designs
- Moulds
- Pardo clay
- Silk screens
- Texture makers

Penny keeps up to date with the latest polymer clay tools, materials, products and accessories and sources them from all over the world. ClayAround only ships to the UK and EU.

Clayground UK
www.clayground.co.uk
The largest UK certified distributer of Cernit clay and craft products by Cernit and Darwi.

GLITTER MAGIC
www.glittermagic.co.uk
Their ultra-fine glitter ranges include Standard, Holographic, Irridescent, and Multimix plus a growing range of glitter kits.

LINDAS ART SPOT on Etsy
www.LindasArtSpot.com
Based in California, America, Linda has some interesting clay accessories.

Resources:

ClayAround Newsletter
On the ClayAround website you can find a link to sign up for the ClayAround newsletter; Penny puts together a selection of videos and links around a particular clay technique or interest each month, and also features polymer clay artists. A really interesting and informative read.

The Blue Bottle Tree
https://thebluebottletree.com

Ginger Davis Allman is the face behind this incredibly useful site. Ginger researches many tools and products associated with polymer clay and writes reports on them so you can make an informed choice. On her site you can find:

- Articles useful for the polymer clay beginner
- Polymer clay tutorials to purchase - knowledge and techniques
- Free polymer clay articles, covering a wide range of techniques, product information, and guidelines
- Sign up to get more free polymer clay information, tips, and offers in your email.

This really is a must-visit site for all polymer clay enthusiasts.

Glossary:

Several times I've been asked what I mean by a word; I've put together a few of the words that might need some further explanation.

Acrylic or metal clay roller:
An acrylic or metal rolling pin for rolling clay into a sheet. If you don't have one of these, a glass jar or bottle can work well.

Ball tool:
A tool with a ball on one or both ends, which can be used in a variety of ways including making texture, adding contours and definition, or smoothing over two clay joins.

Bulls eye cane:
A cane wrapped in a sheet of clay in another colour, or several sheets of colour.

Cane:
A tube of clay, with a pattern that goes all the way along, like a stick of seaside rock. Slices are taken off the cane and used in a variety of ways.

Conditioning:
When clay is in its packet, the various components of the clay can separate. Conditioning is working the clay until it is pliable and does not crack when folded. Not conditioning clay can result in weaker clay that is likely to break easily or crack once cured.

Curing:
Curing is the same as baking, and can be done in a normal oven. Ginger Davis Allman from The Blue Bottle Tree gives a good explanation:

"Polymer clay is PVC powder mixed with plasticizer and some other stuff (fillers, binders, pigment, etc). And as the heat in the oven rises, the PVC particles swell up a bit and soften, eventually fusing into a solid mass that we know as cured polymer clay".

Clay extruder, or Clay gun:
A tool that can create long lengths of clay in a uniformed shape.

Log:
A length of rolled clay, also called a 'snake'.

Mica powder:
Finely ground mica particles that are dyed. When applied to un-cured clay they give a metalic sheen.

Needle tool:
A tool with a long pointed tip which can be used to make bead holes or texture.

Polymer clay:
A type of modelling clay that is primarily polyvinyl chloride (PVC), a plastic. It can be shaped and re-shaped, and needs to be cured (baked) at a low temperature in a normal oven in order to become hard and durable.

Polymer clay adhesive:
There are various types of this, I use Bake & Bond mostly. Polymer clay adhesive can be applied to clay and it will bond cured and non-cured clay when baked.

Skinner blend:
A method of blending two or more colours to make a sheet of smoothly graduated coloured clay. It was developed by Judith Skinner in 1996 and is the basis for most canes.

Tissue blade:
An extremely sharp blade used for cutting and slicing polymer clay; the blades can be flexible, rigid or wavy. The flexible ones are the thinnest and best for cutting extremely thin slices off canes, and the ones I use the most.

CPSIA information can be obtained at www.ICGtesting.com
Printed in the USA
BVIW12n1131180318
510880BV00010B/133